I0080614

UNCONDITIONAL

THE INNOCENCE, BETRAYALS, AND GROWING PAINS

TAWANA ROQUALL FULTZ

Copyright © May 2020 by Tawana Fultz

Copyright © May 2020 by Tawana Roquall Fultz

Publisher: B'ABLE PRODUCTS, LLC

All rights reserved. No part of this publication may be reproduced, distributed, or transmitted in any form or by any means, including photocopying, recording, or other electronic or mechanical methods, without the prior written permission of the publisher, except in the case of brief quotations embodied in critical reviews and certain other noncommercial uses permitted by copyright law.

Published in the United States of America

First Edition, 2021

ISBN: 978-0-578-87221-6

Library of Congress Control Number:

2021905037

Cover by: AILA Designs Media Graphics

Editor: Genevieve A. Scholl

Formatted by: Genevieve A. Scholl

TABLE OF CONTENTS

ACKNOWLEDGEMENTS

First, I would like to acknowledge the King of Kings and Lord of Lords, my Father and Savior Jesus Christ. Without the guidance, wisdom, knowledge, and revelations from our father God, I would not be here today breathing and in my right mind. The purpose of this memoir, my life story, was to give some real-life situations and circumstances a platform for understanding, healing, scriptural and spiritual strategies to encourage yourself or someone else whom may be going through some things as well. With that being said, I give God all the glory for all my experiences because I'm still here and I know now that, "It ain't over until God says it's over!" I want to thank my family for understanding that everything I've been through has made me a stronger woman, and that I am not ashamed of my past, but instead, I am proud of who I am today. Thank you to my four adult children who believe in me and a God that can heal, deliver, and change anybody. I am also grateful for my mother, father, sisters, and everyone that has ever crossed my path and all my trials and tribulations I have experienced, because it caused me to strive to be a woman of virtue, a woman to be loved, honored, and respected for as long as I am on this earth.

INTRODUCTION

Psalm 66:16 KJV

"Come and listen, all you who fear God, and I will tell you what he did for me."

This is a tell-all book based on truth, and is being shared to bring forth another perception and understanding of how life and trauma can change you from one day to another. The innocence, betrayals, and growing pains ultimately shaped and led her to a more positive and intentional lifestyle of total gratefulness. She was born into a very poor and dysfunctional family with abusive, poverty-minded, and criminal drug-related behaviors. Where prostitution and hustling in the streets was practiced, mastered, and "professionalized" before the age of twenty-one. Although the childhood rapes, a failed prison marriage, and four children by four different men left her thoughts of the future unknown, she miraculously, through God's unconditional love and grace, continued to strive and fight to survive a life that was sure to destroy her before she ever finished college. Roquall was her name, and naïve was her game... in the beginning.

THE INNOCENCE

Chapter One

MY INNOCENCE

2 Timothy 1:8 KJV

"Therefore, never be ashamed of the testimony about our Lord or of me, his prisoner. Instead, by God's power, join me in suffering for the sake of the gospel."

Since a toddler, I have always been a soul that loved without limits. From taking in stray animals, to sneaking my hungry or neglected friends into the house and cooking them all the meat my mom had in the freezer. That free, unconditional spirit inside of me always wanted to help. It's a feeling inside of me that sometimes keeps me up at night, worrying about someone or thinking about what I can do to help the people I love.

I spent most of my life with one sister, no brothers, and we were only one year and ten months apart. Being the youngest, I always felt the need to prove to everyone that I was just as smart and responsible as my big sister and some adults. I was very mature for my age and most of my friends were way older than I was. Even my mom's friends would invite me into their conversations for advice. I was well beyond my years and wanted to be treated as such.

When I was about eight years old, there was a lady that lived down the street from us, named Delores. She would always pay me to help her clean her kitchen. After washing all the dishes, I would then sweep and mop the floor before I left. One day she was cooking and, somehow, I ended up making her a salad made with cabbage, bell pepper, onion, and miracle whip. She loved it so much that she started paying me five extra bucks to make it for her at least once a week. From that moment on, for some reason, or another I had a few odd jobs as a kid, from helping the elderly with bags at the grocery stores to cleaning their homes, cooking, or just sitting around having some good, mind-sharpening conversations.

Another one of my odd jobs as a kid was scratching my uncle's scalp. Uncle Big John loved for me to scratch his scalp, and he would pay big bucks for it. He was an exceptionally large man, about 300 pounds, and needed help from time to time. He had bad dandruff and needed it scratched really hard until everything around us was covered in thick white flakes. I know it sounds a bit nasty and it was, but hey, he paid really good. Plus, he was a really fun guy, too. RIP Big John.

I'll never forget the day my grandmother, Ms. Katie Fultz, - R.I.P. September 1, 1911 – April 17, 2010, noticed all of her shoelaces missing from her shoes because I had taken them all out to make leashes for the stray dogs in our neighborhood. She was so mad; she told me to go find a switch from the tree outside, and gave me a whipping like never before. I just wanted to feed and keep them safe so that they wouldn't be run over in the street. Most of my mistakes in life were made mostly because of the unconditional love I have in my heart for others. But never the less, I will continue to live my life as a living sacrifice unto the Lord.

If any of my friends would say they were hungry, I'd cook them all the steak and potatoes we had in the fridge. My mom would come home to cook and all the food would be gone but the kitchen would be spick and span. One time, I even hid a friend in our basement for several nights so she could go to school from my house. I saved all the leftovers from my dinner plate so that she'd have something to eat each night, as well. I wanted to explain to my mom that my friends were either hungry and/or locked out of their houses, but they were mostly too scared to talk about it. I did lots of things to help people, it was just in my nature to serve, be a blessing or of some sort of help to another.

Although helping others brought me joy, the church down the street was even more intriguing to me. It looked kind of scary as I took in the windows and high arches on the roof of the building. Even though I'd never attended Sunday services there, I would have recurring dreams about getting lost there on a secluded floor that hadn't been used in years. The dreams were more like nightmares of me trying to escape but never finding the exit door. I believe those dreams were the beginning of my fascination with the church and what went on inside.

I actually got hit by a car down the street from that church, though it was kind of funny. I was riding my bike in the street. Of course, I had been told not to do so, but I tried to cross the street anyway to the other side. A car came out of nowhere and hit my bike, sending me and it high in the sky. I can still see the bike wheel flying in the air. Immediately after the hit, I jumped up off the ground and started running as fast as I could back to the house.

Once I made it to my front porch and looked back, the driver of the car was right behind me. He wanted to talk to my mom and make sure I was alright. I jumped up and down, then spun around, begging the man not to talk to my mom. I was afraid that she would know that I was riding my bike in the street and I would get a whipping and punishment. I begged him, "Please? Please sir? Look at me! I'm fine!" However, my mom eventually came to the door and listened to the man as he explained what happened.

As they looked and checked me over, we noticed my ear was hanging halfway off my head. It was bleeding and I had a few more scrapes and scratches here and there. My mom thanked the man for checking on me and notifying her as well. She wasn't mad at me at all as I expected and after I was cleaned up and safe again, she allowed me to sit with her in the house the remainder of that day. I guess she was assuring that I did not fall asleep for the next few hours. My ear healed up just fine without stitches.

At that time, we lived in a three-family flat. We had one of the two apartments upstairs, and there was one large apartments on the lower level. My mom and the lady downstairs were married to brothers, which made us all family except for the other upstairs tenant across from us. But she was just as close as family. They would all get together in the large apartment downstairs, at the table to drink, smoke or to simply get dressed to go to a party.

All of us kids, nine years old and younger, would stay together until they would return or played in the bedroom when they just partied in the living room. Most of the times they would leave beer, liquor bottles, cups, and ashtrays behind filled with everything they had been consuming. We would pour all the swigs they left behind at the bottom of each liquor bottle or cup into one container. Then we would gather all the butts in the ashtrays, roll them all up into one and have our own little party as well. This was the very moment I began tasting alcohol and marijuana! It wasn't till later I learned to smoke cigarettes.

Shortly after, we moved from that area to the west side of Detroit. Again, I noticed another huge church two block up from our new home and something kept making me want to go. I would get up every Sunday morning, get dressed all by myself, and walk right into the church, find a seat, and sit there until the service ended. I was only around eight or nine years old and no one ever asked me where my parents were. I just loved church service and always dreamed of singing in a church choir one day.

Unconditional: The Innocence, Betrayals, and Growing Pains

Unfortunately, the smoking continued with my first best friend, named Doll Baby, who lived right next door to us. Doll had a cousin that came over to her house often. When she'd come, she'd always have weed (marijuana) or was drinking something. She was a few years older than us. Doll and I would walk around to her house a few streets up and smoke weed with her every time she came around.

At this house, was where I met my first boyfriend, Ron. He was in my sixth-grade class. Every girl in the neighborhood knew this boy and his brothers, too. The brothers were mixed nationalities - part Indian and part African-American, so they had this long, curly, black hair. Everyone wanted to play in their long, black, curly hair and they all resembled the singer Prince!

Ron was such a sweetheart! He would walk me home from school every day and help with all my household chores after school. My sister thought it was amazing that he would be cleaning toilets and mopping floors at our house all the time, just for me. I will never forget Ron. He was the first boy to ever spoil me. Those middle school days were fun but ruff as well.

My sixth and seventh grade years left two scars in me that I will never forget. First, a classmate of mine was brutally killed and I had nightmares for years about her and still do to this day! Her name was Shakira. I can still hear the PA from the school Principal as we took a moment of silence for her in class that morning.

Shakira stayed home that day because she was not feeling well as her mom left for work. Apparently, some friends of the family came by to rob the house that day unknowingly that Shakira was inside the home alone. They entered and once they noticed Shakira was there, they began to rape and strangle her until she was unconscious. They then proceeded to place her tied-up body in the closet and set it on fire. It was the most horrific thing I had ever known.

The so-called longtime friends of the family were eventually caught and had given statements during the trial that I will never forget. One guy explained that after he had seen her, he panicked and didn't know what to do. He then stated that he couldn't live with himself knowing what he did to her and didn't want her to tell. "I had to kill her because I couldn't let her tell," he had explained. Shakira was raped, tied up, strangled with an extension cord, placed in a closet, and burnt beyond recognition. It's still a daunting feeling to this day when I think about the excuses the men gave for killing that sweet, innocent, precious little girl.

The second unforgettable scar that year, happened when I was staring out the window in my sixth-grade classroom. It was a sight that I feel no child should ever have to see. I was sitting there in class daydreaming as the teacher taught her lesson for the day. I then noticed a man and woman walking down the street together, arguing. The man grabbed the woman by her collar and seemed to be dragging her down the street by her hair, right passed my classroom window. As my vision zeroed in on them, I noticed that it was my mother and her boyfriend!

Immediately, I began to try to distract all the kids in class. I was so afraid someone would see them and call police or make fun of them. My heart was racing so fast! I wanted to run out and help my mom, but I also didn't want anyone to see them. I watched until I couldn't see them any longer from the window, lowered my head down to the desk, and began to worry and imagine what could possibly be the problem. Thank God that relationship was short lived!

Another move further west in the City of Detroit was very much welcomed and was the beginning of a stable life at home with mom and my older sister. It was the first home my mom had ever purchased. We lived in a brick side-by-side corner townhouse. Even though my sister was only one year and ten months older than I was, we never seemed to get along much but I loved her and wanted to be the closest thing to her most of the time. My sister and I managed to meet quite a few people on our block from just walking around the neighborhood and back and forth to the store.

During those years, I started playing the violin, the saxophone and began strengthening my vocals. The saxophone was so sexy to me, so I played both alto and tenor sax. The choir was another thing I loved, but I also enjoyed being a cute cheerleader during my high school basketball games as well. But what I was mostly known for was my singing. I love to sing, and it is how I find my peace and keep my joy.

My relationship with my mom was good, but I had a hard time obeying some of her rules due to lack of understanding, of course. My mind told me that as long as I got good grades and did my chores, I should have been able to do pretty much whatever I wanted. My friends were always much older than I was, and I wanted to sit and chill at their houses for as long as I wanted. Especially because my friends' houses were either right down the street from ours, on the same block or immediately around the corner.

I did a lot of staying out past my curfew and/or not coming home at all. Again, I was right down the street, and did I say I was an excellent straight-A student? But most of the time I was at my BFF Crystal's house, who lived behind my house but across the street and a few houses down. Crystal was at least five to six years older than me, with two babies, but she had her own house. There was also a couple that lived down the street that I would go and sit with for hours, which eventually led to smoking cigarettes, weed, and drinking beer later on down the line.

Other days, I hung out with two girls that lived almost directly across the street from us named Tonya and Niecy. They also had a little brother named Antwan. Their mother was such a sweet lady and always invited me to church with them every Sunday. I loved going to church with them, and afterwards, they'd go eat dinner at their grandma's house. Their church was a bit strict but I loved going with them and I also loved singing everyday with Tonya.

There was a strong spiritual connection to me in the church that drew me in like a magnetic. I believed nothing was impossible and everything was possible with the help of thy Lord and Savior, Jesus Christ. The teachings of Christ's unconditional love were the very things that saved my life and changed my prospective on life forever.

Chapter Two

STOLEN VIRTUE

Jeremiah 29:11 KJV

"For I know the plans I have for you," declares the Lord, "plans to prosper you and not to harm you, plans to give you hope and a future."

I was a good girl up until high school. I can still remember my first day. It was called zero-hour, and, in that hour, you were given your class schedule for the year. You were also allowed to change your classes if you wanted to. It was not a full day of classes and most of the kids were meeting up often at the nearby Coney Island for lunch.

Leaving the school for lunch and any other interests was how I spent my days. After a while, a life of skipping classes, "parlaying" with friends, drinking and smoking (marijuana) was all I did from day to day.

Eventually, I met a man named Popeye, who lived in the apartment building, across the street, behind the school football field. Popeye was at least ten years older than I was and he had his own apartment with his brother. He would allow me and my friends to skip class at his apartment and buy alcohol for us from the liquor store next door.

He did have a girlfriend, but she was not there most of the time. After spending so much time there during school hours, I began to notice how much he smoked cigarettes. It was amusing to me to see the smoke circles he would make when blowing the smoke out his mouth. One day I just asked him to let me try. I took my first puff and choked so hard, I became determined to successfully inhale and make smoke circles as he did. Between the ages of fourteen and fifteen was when I began smoking cigarettes.

At about 15 years old, I remember seeing all the teens outside just standing around the building. They were riding around the school in circles in their new cars their parents got them or just hanging around skipping classes. It was the last day of school before Christmas break, and I decided that me and my friend, Nunie, would skip class and stand outside with the others. While standing on the sidewalk, I observed some guys riding around the school with loud music and thought I would like to ride with them because it looked cool to have a car.

Nunie was hesitant about getting into the car with these guys, of course, since we'd just met. Nunie was worried about her brother seeing her get into the car and telling on her later. I begged her to get in and insisted that we were just going to circle around the school a few times to be seen by all the fly girls and then we'd go back to class.

Feeling that these two guys looked innocent and friendly, we got into the car. After riding around the school twice, I noticed the driver make a wrong turn and head for the highway.

I immediately asked where he was going? They assured us that we were just going to their house really quick and to not be scared. They said we were too scary and acting like virgins. I tried to play it cool and not seem too paranoid when we arrived at the house.

They asked us to come in, and Nunie and I said, "No thanks. We have to hurry back to school."

The guys began to tease us for being scared to go into the house. It was very cold in the car and after about five minutes, we decided to go into the house. Once we were inside and about to sit down at the dining table, a guy came from the basement to lock the side door.

He stated, "Okay. Now, let's stop fronting and get this party started!" Nunie and I both looked at each other with fear in our eyes. We knew we were in big trouble.

We were both virgins and had never seen a boy in his underwear. There were four guys total in the house and two of them were walking around in their underwear. They then separated us by taking Nunie to a bedroom and me to the basement. There was one with me in the basement and three upstairs in the room with Nunie. The one guy in the basement with me was telling me that if I had sex with him, he would make sure that the other guys didn't touch me. All I could think about was my family.

With my eyes closed tight, I could picture their faces in my mind as I tried to telepathically send them a message through the images in my head. Wishing they could hear me and save me from what was about to happen. After a few minutes, he begin to take off my clothes and proceeds to have intercourse with me for about ten minutes. After he was done, he immediately grabbed all my clothes and ran upstairs. I was sitting on the bed in the basement, thinking I should try to get out of the side door. But then I remembered there was about six feet of snow outside and I had no shoes or clothes on.

I was so afraid I would freeze to death. I could hear my friend Nunie screaming and begging for them to stop. My heart was so heavy that I was the one who begged her to get in the car with these guys. So, I then crept up the stairs to the side door and began to unlock it. As I unlocked the first lock, I could hear Nunie scream out again, except this time it was like the wailing of a mother losing a child. It was so painful to hear. Immediately, I thought to myself, "I got her in this mess; I better die with her". So, I went back down in the basement and sat back down on the bed and waited for them to come back to kill me, too.

After several hours of torture and humiliation, the two guys that brought us there took us back to the car and started driving us to another one of their friend's house. They tried to get Nunie to get out of the car and go inside. We begged and pleaded no! And eventually they got back in the car and stated that they were taking us back to school and when we got out, we better not look back at them or they would shoot us in the back and kill us.

We arrived at the school, we didn't look back and ran into the school. We both called our parents and they came to pick us up. Later, three of the guys were caught and prosecuted after a long and humiliating trial. All but the one who raped me, He was never caught. Nunie and I have remained friends still to this day.

My high school days were not all bad, though I did a lot of interesting things during that time as well. I met a girl in high school named, LaVette. She was known for dancing on this old show called The New Dance Show, here in the City of Detroit.

One day, she invited me to go with her on the show and I did. I believe I was in two or three recordings. It was so funny, because I had nothing to wear and I ended up wearing my mom's grey double-breasted dress.

My head was shaved on one side with my initials engraved in the back. Dancing was and is not my best talent and I was just shaking and moving. Because of the recording, we were told to keep dancing nonstop for the entire broadcast which lasted about thirty minutes straight. Believe it or not, it was hard trying to dance and still look good until the commercial break.

That was a fun time, we were making up all kinds of moves to keep the camera in our direction. Now, by the end of high school, things started to get complicated again. Popeye and I were still just friends until one day he finally made his move on me. I will never forget; we were just chilling at his house smoking weed and drinking beer. All of a sudden, he started to kiss me. I liked Popeye; he was incredibly attractive. So, yeah, I kissed him back.

Popeye was fine and had thin curly hair with light hazel eyes, but his teeth were a mess. Again, he was at least ten to twelve years older than me. I was only like fifteen at the time and we were in his bedroom just watching TV. After he kissed me, I began to get very moist down there and hot as a firecracker! Ugh! It was a very sloppy kiss, but I thought I was ready for it!

He began to pull my pants down and started rubbing his hand on my private area. I was so wet, it felt like I had peed a little. The moment he pulled his business out and started rubbing it on my vagina, I got scared and started to panic! All I could see was my mom's face in my mind just shaking her head. Immediately, I jumped up, having changed my mind, apologized to him, and got the hell out of there as fast as I could. I didn't go back over to his apartment for a while after that. I tried going back to school and getting myself together.

I was doing good for a while until I decided to skip class to go with my friend to get her a pregnancy test. We both had a Vo-tech class together around lunch time and decided to get off the school bus and go to the pregnancy clinic down the street from our Vo-Tech Building. Once we arrived at the clinic, my friend started filling out the necessary paperwork to start the test. The nurse then took my friend back to the testing area and told me I was not allowed to go back with her. So, I decided that I would complete the paperwork for myself so that I could go back there with her. I lied about a missed period and sexual activities that never happened.

Once I was called back in the testing area with my friend, I peed and gave blood for testing. After about 30 minutes, the nurse came back in and called a handful of people, including my friend, and told them to follow her. Then she came back to the group I was waiting with and stated that everyone of us had a positive test result. I was so upset at the time because I knew for sure that I had never had sex before. I'd thought about it with Popeye, but I never went through with it.

I began to get irate and rude with the nurse as she spoke to the group. When she walked away, I gathered everyone and told them to not trust their pregnancy results. I reassured them that I was a virgin and never had sex willingly before in my life. I even told them to rally with me to have the clinic shut down for false results. I was livid and I was determined to prove them wrong about my test results!

A few weeks later, I started to feel weird while I was walking to school, eating a delicious breakfast sandwich. As the butter from the eggs was dripping down my hand, I began to feel a little queasy and started throwing up everything I had swallowed. I continued to walk to the school, confused as to why I threw up. Later on, that night, I began to think about that morning's sickness. It then dawned on me what that nurse had said to me about my test results.

25

So, I ran upstairs to the bathroom, locked the door, and started staring at myself in the mirror. The longer I stared, the more my eyes began to well up. I couldn't have been pregnant. I didn't even have sex with Popeye. All he did was rubbed his penis on me and I stopped it. What in the heck was going on with me right now?

Moments later, my mom called me downstairs for something. I used to play with my mom all the time about being pregnant because she was so afraid of it happening to my sister and me. This time when I walked into the kitchen to see what she had wanted, I tried to play that game with her again. Only I couldn't smile at that moment and instead tears started to run down my face and I ran back upstairs into the bathroom. My mom knew then that it was not a game this time.

We eventually sat down to talk about it, and I tried to reassure her that I did not have sex with anyone. I told her all about Popeye and how I saw her face and decided not to have sex with him. She seemed to not believe me and was disappointed. I believe my mom gave me the silent treatment for weeks. I was sure that my mom wanted me to have an abortion, and after I told Popeye about the pregnancy, he cried.

Popeye knew I was too young, but it was his first child and he wanted to raise the baby by himself. My mom threatened to press charges against him for rape because I was only fifteen and he was so much older than me. After a few weeks of all the conflict and confusion, I just wanted my mom back the way we used to be. Eventually, my mom took me to the doctor and had me tested and examined. The doctor told her I was pregnant, but he could not tell if I had been having sex.

I begged my mom to believe me that I did not have sex with anyone. This was the first time I felt betrayed by my family because nobody ever believed me. I eventually agreed to have the abortion that my mom set up for me. The thought of killing a baby was sad and scary, but I knew I was too young to be having a baby. The abortion was very painful. I screamed so loud, you could hear the walls echoing my voice down the hallways.

One part of me wanted to be angry and sad, but the other part of me just wanted my mommy back, and for things around the house to get back to normal. We hadn't laughed, smiled, or just chit chat with one another for a while since I became pregnant. Afterward, my mom entered my recovery room with a balloon and a small teddy bear in her hands. We went home and things did get better for a short while. However, there's more.

If I hadn't been through enough already, several months later, I almost got kidnapped! I was walking down the street while coming home from the corner store. An older man pulled up on the side of the road and said, "Get in this car now!"

I was only fifteen, so I looked around to see if he was talking to someone else. There was no one there but me and I asked, "What?"

He said again, "Get in this car!"

"Sir, I'm only 15 years old. and I don't know you."

As I started to walk faster, he jumped out of his car, yelling, "You my wife, and I said come here now!" and began chasing me.

I started running, until I saw the house where a lady and cute puppy lived with her front door open, so I ran into her house, closed her door, and locked it. The lady came from the back room and said, "What is going on?"

I said, "Please help me! This old man says I'm his wife but I'm only 15 years old. I don't know him! Please call my mom!"

He began beating on her door, screaming, "Let my wife out! Give me my wife!"

I begged her, "Please don't open that door. Please!"

She said let me talk to him ok. She opened the door, "Sir, this is a child. She is not your wife!"

He tried to push through her door and almost knocked her on the floor, and we both struggled to get the door closed and locked again.

She yelled through the door, "I'm calling the police! Get off my porch!"

She then called the police and my mom. The old man had left before either one of them had shown up. As my mom and I walked back around the corner together, I remember seeing my own shadow on the ground. It scared me so bad, I screamed and ran into the house.

That day I could've been kidnapped forever or even killed, but God didn't see fit to let my life end there. Moreover, I will never forget how the Lord keeps on delivering me out of the hands of potential enemies.

Chapter Three

STOLEN AGAIN

Psalm 10:14 KJV
"But you, God, see the trouble of the afflicted; you consider their grief and take it in hand. The victims commit themselves to you; you are the helper of the fatherless."

A time period of about seven-eight months had past until the second sexual assault by a close relative's baby daddy occurred. It was almost the end of all family relations and connections. It all began when I had decided to delay my punishment for staying out the night before and hiding when my mom came to pick me up. I actually begged the couple whose house I was at to lie to my mom and say I was not there.

Christy was about 35 years old and a little short, white female with a long ponytail down her back that swung across her butt when she walked. Her boyfriend, Derrick, was a tall, black man of about 38 years old. Christy's house was the neighborhood party spot every day in the summertime. Christy would buy beers and cigarettes and let us smoke and drink with her all day. It was where I could see the guy I liked that lived around the corner from us. He was friends with Derrick.

One day, my mom came looking for me down to Christy's house. I was inside drinking and didn't want to leave at that time. So, I had begged Christy not to open the door and to be quiet until my mom had left. Christy was a nervous wreck and almost gave in. Eventually, my mom left, threatening to call the police.

I insisted on staying and spending the night so I could spend more time with the guy from around the corner. After a long, fun night with my neighbors, I decided to go home... after my mom had left for work of course. I just wanted to take a quick shower, change into some clean clothes, and think about how I was going to get ready for my punishment or if I really wanted to stick around for it.

While at the house, taking a shower, I had heard my cousin come in from out of town with her boyfriend. She and her brother had lived with us before but only for a short time. I asked her when she was leaving and if I could go back with her to avoid my punishment. She told me that she was not going back right now but her boyfriend was returning in a couple days. I decided to leave with him just for a few days, and besides, I'd always wanted to meet his brother that was being released from juvenile detention the next day, so that added to my excuses to leave.

My cousin told me to stay home and don't leave town because my mom would be even more mad if she found out I left the state as well. I was only sixteen or seventeen at the time. I left anyway, and the moment I arrived, I was given a half ounce of marijuana. He then left to go hustle and was gone the entire day. His sister and I sat and smoked all day and night until I eventually went upstairs to sleep.

Their house was kind of bare and there was no visible place to sleep comfortably. They had roaches, and I refused to sleep on the floor. Because he was gone in the streets, selling drugs all day and all night, I decided that I'd sleep in his bed at least until he got home. Well, he came home in the early morning and I didn't hear him come in. Of course, I was high as a kite from smoking all that weed he had given his sister and I earlier that day.

All I can remember is him climbing on top of me, grabbing my hands and holding me down on the bed. He tried to kiss me and stick his tongue in my mouth. I began to bite down really hard on my lips tucked tightly into my mouth. While trying to force his tongue through my lips, he used one hand to pull down my pants. All I could think was that his mom and sister were downstairs sleeping and if I could wake them up, they would not believe me and not take me back home to Michigan.

I was so afraid to be out of the state by myself with them and no money or nothing to get back home. It was only months after the first rape when they took my virginity. I began to tell myself to do what I did last time to make it home safe. I gave him a struggle but he did eventually get his tiny little penis inside me a bit. It was so small I barely even felt it while I was still preventing him from kissing me and sticking his tongue inside my mouth.

32

The next day, he was able to buy me a bus ticket home. After getting the ticket and going to the loading area, he actually tried to kiss me on the cheek to say goodbye. I held my ticket tightly in my hand as I pulled away. I returned home and tried to forget it ever happened. About a year later, my cousin's boyfriend was sentenced to ten years in prison for another crime unrelated to me and I felt justice was served and never spoke or thought of it again.

A few years after that rape occurred, my cousin and I had got into a fight while I was pregnant with my first child. It was in my apartment when the argument started. Somehow, we were talking about how stupid each other was for being with the men we had in the past. It was a touchy subject, because I was pregnant and a single mother and so was she. The father of my baby was not involved in the pregnancy nor did he want to be a part of my child's life.

At some point, I grabbed a wooden two by four for protection while telling her to get out of my apartment. She grabbed the wooden stick and we pulled back and forth. During the struggle, the stick hit me in the stomach and I became angrier. I wanted to hurt her as bad as she hurt me. So, I told her that her baby daddy wasn't any good either and that she was in love with a man that had no penis!

Oh boy! Did that open a can of worms that I really did not want! Of course I tried to take it back and tell the real truth about the whole situation. That was when other family members had to put their two cents in. But I'm afraid it was too late for that. I tried to explain to several family members that, yes, I said it out of anger, but yeah, I was actually raped by my cousin's baby daddy. My cousin eventually said that she believed me and was terribly upset with her baby daddy for taking advantage of me in the first place.

Surprisingly, after about thirty years, I received a friend request from this man on one of my social media sites I often visit. I was upset and offended at the nerve of the man after he did what he did to me. I couldn't, for the life of me, figure out why he thought it was okay to request me on social media. The request only re-triggered the anger I had inside for him. I began to feel the pain of that rape again. I started praying and fasting for some kind of clarity or understanding of why I was reliving that time in my life all over again.

Moreover, I realized that I had some unresolved issues still simmering in my heart. I asked my cousin and other family members their thoughts on how they felt about the rape story. It was very surprising to hear that a few of my family members stated they felt it was my fault for leaving with the man in the first place. There seemed to be only but a few whom believed in me, and that made me furious! This was the second time I felt betrayed by my family, and it became clear to me to let go of any and every one that called me a liar and to make sure they would never be considered family of mine again!

I then confronted everyone who was supposedly in disbelief because I felt it was completely cruel to question someone's rape.

Needing a fresh new start, I began looking into a Job Corps Training Program, an alternative school for teenaged kids in Edinburg, Indiana.

Chapter Four

MY FIRST LOVE

1 John 4:1 KJV

"Dear friends, do not believe everyone who claims to speak by the Spirit. You must test them to see if the spirit they have comes from God. For there are many false prophets in the world."

Edinburg, Indiana, Atterbury Job Corps, was like a live-in college campus, where you could get your G.E.D. and learn some skills for job readiness. I went to Job Corps because I was behind in high school, and I also wanted to join a few friends there who had recently left. 1989 was the year I met my husband, Trent Braxton. It was a twelve-hour bus ride from Detroit to Edinburg, Indiana. At that time, I was a bit loud, but innocent and loved to wear dresses all the time.

When I arrived at the orientation building, I noticed my husband immediately. I can remember watching him from afar. He had on a green and white striped shirt with green denim jeans and some green and white stripped adidas gym shoes. I stared at him for a while before I leaned over to the girl next to me and whispered, "Girl, look at him. Now that's the kind of guy I want to marry". He was handsome, sexy, macho, and dressed very nice. He seemed perfect to me, and I was melting like butter, while watching him interact with others.

Although he was still a student there, he was also an orientation monitor working in the building where we were waiting to get permanent dorm rooms assigned. They had a basketball game that night and the new (Oreos) orientation were not allowed to attend until after they were placed in housing. Somehow, he ended up asking me to go with him to the game and he pretended to be touring me around the campus. I had a great time with him, though I had the butterflies every time he looked at me. After the basketball game, things started to go left again for me.

Apparently, he had many admirers there at the campus and they were not going to let me have him at all. Soon after I was placed in my dorm room, I started getting write ups. My room was being destroyed every day after I left for class. My mattress would be thrown off the bed and there was trash all over the floor. They even spray painted the wall over my bed, "B** go home!" I never knew who was doing this to me, but I knew it was jealousy because Trent walked me to class and carried my books for me every day.

One day after class, I was walking down the hall in my building and this girl bumped me really hard. At this time, I was so fed up with the bullying that I was ready to fight anyone. I tried to keep walking but another came and bumped me really hard again. I stopped and pulled the knife out of my jacket pocket. "If anyone wants to fight me, well, come and get it!" I yelled. "I'm tired of this mess! I'm ready to handle whatever problems you got with me!"

All of a sudden, girls started coming from every direction, surrounding me, calling me names, and trying to get close enough to hit me. I began swinging that knife like crazy to keep them away from me. The security guards came and were trying to take the knife from my hand, but the girls were still getting closer and closer to me. There was not enough security to keep the girls off me, so I continued to fight for the knife for dear life! Thank God! The guards only suffered a few minor cuts and abrasions and did not pursue anything further other than an immediate suspension and transport back to Michigan. I continued to see Trent off and on during his home visits in Michigan.

Once I arrived home, I eventually started dating my first child's father, and when Trent was able to come into town, we would go on double dates together because neither one of us had cars. We would go on double dates and leave our dates at the table and sneak into the bathroom to have sex and put passion marks on each other's necks. We'd come back to the table and laugh at how our dates never even noticed anything. Because Trent was in and out of town so much, we were never seriously committed, so, eventually, I ended up moving in with my date and would become pregnant with my first child by the age of eighteen.

My first move-in situation did not last very long at all and ended on my eighteenth birthday. I planned a birthday party for the day of our move out because I wanted to go out with a bang after we decided to go our separate ways. I invited anybody and everybody! I was sure to have the place packed. And, boy, was it packed alright. I had never seen so many men together in one apartment before in my life! It was about seventy-five guys and me!

Every time a car filled with women pulled up, the guys would get so excited, they'd run them off. After a while, the guys were demanding some excitement though I was in heaven! Pictures of outfits started coming to mind and I began to change into them. I then instructed the DJ of my all-time favorites playlist and began to dance from the window to the wall! I cleaned up! Money was flying everywhere!

The DJ played my favorite, "Ain't No Future in Yo Front in," about twenty times as I danced and pranced all over them negros until I had no more hiding places to put my money. It was the best eighteenth birthday ever! It was never intended to be just me and a room full of men with money, it was supposed to be a normal birthday party. But baby, it was a day I will never forget.

Eventually, I moved into another apartment before having my baby. My child was only three weeks old when Trent came back and finally moved in with me. We were becoming serious after about three years of knowing each other. It was amazing having him there with my son and me. He brought me out of my shell and taught me how to love openly, honestly, and passionately.

Unconditional: The Innocence, Betrayals, and Growing Pains

One day, Trent and I were laughing and dancing in the living room, getting ready for a party, and out of excitement, Trent jumped up and stomped his feet really hard on the floor and sprained his ankle. His ankle had swollen so fast he could not put his shoes on. I was excited to hang out with our mutual old Job Corps friends, and they were on their way. Trent had to tell them that he was not going, but insisted he wanted us to go on and enjoy ourselves. My son was already with the sitter and I really didn't want to waste a kid-free night. Although I went and had a great time, I left Trent at home babysitting my bird and his painful swollen ankle.

When I returned home from the party, the bird was dead and he was apologizing, saying he blew a little weed smoke in his face. Till this day, I still wish I would have stayed home to protect my bird but also take care of Trent's ankle. I really did love him like that, and to this day, I still can't believe he let me go out, dressed like that, with two men and didn't try to stop me at all.

Later, I would accidently rub up against his ankle over and over again while trying to move around in the house. I will never forget the moment he sat me down and described how painful it was when his ankle was moved or hit accidently. He explained to me that if I had an ankle like that, he would get up slowly when near me and ensure proper distance to not agitate my ankle at all costs. I finally understood that kind of care was intentional and only happened when you disciplined

40

yourself to love on purpose. I never accidentally hit that ankle again. Thanks Trent!

However, we were both unemployed, struggling financially, and living in my subsidized low-income apartment with a new baby, which made it difficult for us to move forward productively as a family. So, one day, we both decided that I would buy drugs and he would re-sell them for profit. I guess he had sold drugs before and we knew a lot of drug addicts in the apartment complex. Once I got the drugs and he cut and bagged them up, Trent began to go out and sell to our neighbors. After about a month or so, we were invited to a party at another apartment close by.

All I can remember about that party is, we were playing cards having a great time. Next thing I knew, I woke up about 7pm the next evening, fully dressed, soaking wet in my bed alone. I woke up, puzzled, wondering why I was wet in my clothes and Trent was nowhere to be found. I got up and went into the living room, looking for my keys, money, and Trent. My son was still at the sitter's house.

I couldn't find anything, so I ran next door to my neighbor's apartment whom we were with the night before and asked her what had happened. She said Trent left to make a sale and I passed out at the party, so they brought me home and put me in the shower, trying to wake me up and then put me in my bed. I immediately started calling around, looking for Trent, my money, my gun, and the keys to my apartment. After no luck finding Trent, I got a phone call from Trent's mom.

She was cursing me like never before about giving her son drugs. She said in so many words that Trent had been battling a drug addiction for years and had no business handling, selling, or using any kind of drugs. She then explained that Trent was found in the closet of his brother's house, screaming and crying, trying to kill himself with my gun and would not come out for hours. Trent had smoked all of the crack we had to sell and was going crazy. After the high finally began to wear off they were able to get the gun away from him and they took him to the mental hospital for detoxification and suicide watch.

I went to visit him there for a few weeks until he was released in the care of his mom. We continued to see each other, and one day while he was at my apartment in Taylor, some girl he dated from job corps arrived at his mom's house looking for him. Trent's mom called and told him someone was at her house, from out of town looking for him. After we found out who she was, he immediately told her to go back home because he was with me. She refused to leave his mom's house until she talked to him about some unfinished business they had out of state.

He told her he would talk with her another time as it was getting late and we were getting ready for bed at the time. Considering she had driven many hours to Detroit for her first time, Trent's mom told her she could stay the night to get some sleep before the drive back to her hometown. The next day, Trent's mom called again, saying, "Come home, son. I think something's wrong with her and she can't drive home right now." We thought the girl was just faking to get him back there, so he refused again and told her to go back home. Trent's mom told her to go to the hospital if she was not feeling well.

After a while of her not getting up off the couch, Trent's mom called 911. She was taken to the hospital and was pronounced dead shortly after. After three weeks of her family trying to understand what had happened. They began trying to press charges against Trent for the murder of their daughter. Although it took weeks for the autopsy to come back, it showed that the girl had a rare blood disorder. The blood disorder could not have been detected and it was sudden and there was nothing anyone could have done to save her.

Trent mourned and cried on my shoulder for weeks while I tried my best to be supportive as possible. It was hard to see the man I loved cry and go through fits over another woman he had dated. But her passing was so unexpected and sad for me as well. I thought we were getting through it together until, one day, I got a phone call from his mom, stating that Trent was in jail and he wanted her to give me his information so that I could write him or come visit.

Trent had been arrested for armed robbery and facing some hard time if convicted. After several court appearances and trial hearings, Trent was sentenced to nine to twenty years in prison.

Chapter Five

THE SIDE HUSTLE

2 Chronicles 7:14

"If my people, who are called by my name, will humble themselves and pray and seek my face and turn from their wicked ways, then I will hear from heaven, and I will forgive their sin and will heal their land."

Shortly after, I lost my apartment in Taylor and I moved in with my sister, where I began babysitting for some friends of hers that were exotic female strippers at a night club. After seeing all that money, helping them separate and count it, I began going to the club with them. Trying to find ways to make more money, I would watch their money on the stage, keep their purses, and make runs if they needed me too. Because I was living with my sister, I decided that I wanted to get on stage and get some of that money, too, so I could save up for another apartment for me and my son.

Tricking to survive started at an early age for me because I wanted to be grown well before my time. About sixteen, or maybe even seventeen, I needed a place to stay and a friend of mine allowed me to stay at her house. The weird part about that was she was tricking with her own child's grandfather and told me I had to, too, in order to buy my own hygiene products and food. The man was married, and he was about seventy years old.

I needed the money, so she called him up and told him about me. We decided he would eat my sandwich for one hundred and fifty dollars. Just enough to buy the things I needed at the time. Maybe a day or two later, he came by and picked me up. We drove to his apartment where him and his wife lived.

He walked me to the bed and asked me to remove my bottoms. As I removed my pants, he reached across the bed and grabbed a pillow and sat me down on the bed and placed the pillow under my butt. I will never forget that feeling, as it was kind of funny, because I didn't know what an orgasm felt like so I fought like hell to stop shaking and keep still. Afterward, he only gave me one hundred dollars because he said that I didn't relax and enjoy myself.

Somehow, I managed to end up in some of the most compromising situations and circumstances. I remember when I tried to hustle out of my apartment until that particular situation showed me that I was not about that life and I had kids to live for. I had walked across the street from my apartment to speak with a neighbor. As I began to walk back to my apartment, I noticed some shadows moving around inside my apartment. I quickly backed into my friend's apartment and ran to her window to see what I could observe.

Unconditional: The Innocence, Betrayals, and Growing Pains

There was about twelve people in my apartment, shopping as if I had invited them. An old friend of mine was mad at me about not getting a purchase she wanted and decided to kick my door in and take what I had. I was livid as I watched them destroy my things, and it was that day I had to walk away from those hustle and flow crimes all together. In order to get even with those whom kicked my door in, I would have had to kill about twelve people. I was not trying to be no mass murderer, so I politely moved from the area and walked away with my freedom and my life.

The struggle lived on but so did I, and I was also determined to survive one way or another. So, one day, I was walking to the corner store to get a few groceries. My pantry and refrigerator were both bare, although my kids were away for the summer with their dads. It was weird to me that my kids were gone and I still couldn't even afford to feed myself. That was the moment I realized that my kids and government assistance was taking care of me and not me taking care of them as much as I thought.

It was the hungriest I think I had ever been in life. I was so broke that I had gathered some return bottles and a handful of pennies to walk to the grocery store to see if I could get bread and whatever else I could get to eat. I was literally eating from a pinto bean can. Only eating three to ten beans every so many hours so that it would last the whole day. I had just moved into the apartment in Pontiac and the guy, Roddy, who

I was working with at the time, did a disappearance act on me to save his family and relationship.

As I was walking to the corner store, a guy pulled up in a car alongside me and started to ask me my name. I tried to brush him off quickly and walk faster. I yelled back at him that I didn't talk to men in the street. He proceeded to pull over and park his car in the store parking lot. He told me that I was beautiful and he wanted to know what I felt like. I told him I was offended and proceeded into the store. I tried to hurry with my purchase because I had a lot of change and a bag of bottles in my hand.

This guy then walked up and said, "I got it. Anything else you need?" I grabbed some potatoes, because it was the item I needed most. He then stated to the cashier, "And add some condoms on this order," and then placed a case of beer on the counter.

I turned to him to ask, "What are the condoms for?"

He replied, "For you. Told you that we getting busy after we get back to your apartment." He paid for my things, and I proceeded to walk out the door when he asked if I wanted a ride back.

I told him no and that I was fine walking. He followed alongside me to my apartment, insisting that he help me with the bags I was carrying. After arriving to my apartment door, I dropped some of my groceries on the ground while trying to put the keys in the door lock. I finally opened the door and he followed behind me, placing my groceries on the dining room table. After placing the food on the table, he pulled out his wallet and about five hundred dollars and laid it on the table then sat down.

I looked at him and immediately grabbed the money off the table and took it back to my room. I stopped at the bathroom on my way back to the dining area, did a quick wash at the sink, and came back to the table where he was sitting, placing the condom on his private area. I shook my head and sat down on him backward as he sat in the chair. All I could think about was how I really needed that five hundred dollars and what I was going to do with it.

He left about fifteen minutes after. I did get his name and number, but only saw him one other time after that encounter, and it was only to drop some more money to me in hopes for the next rendezvous that never happened. For some strange reason, I had been propositioned in so many different ways by so many different types of men that it felt like I was walking around with a for sale sign of my forehead. Men had always been overly aggressive with me from as far back as I could remember and it made me feel like if I had to deal with the disregard and disrespect, then I must make them pay. Although I came from a family with a long history of prostitution, it was only an option chosen in life-or-death situations.

My very first night on stage was at an all-white bar called Henry the V111. Me and a friend decided to audition there first because we were afraid of the black crowd. Knowing we had some imperfections, and I didn't have the boobs nor backside as the other girls had. We thought if the white men loved us then we would gain the courage to dance in front of the black crowd. The black bars seemed to be very judgmental, and I wasn't ready for them yet. I will never forget how scared I was to get on that stage half-naked. The first song played and we were to dance in full costume, during the second song, we had to take off our tops, and we were allowed to come down off the stage and start the lap dancing on the customers in the club for the third song.

After my first night, the manager came to me and gave me my weekly schedule to come in and start dancing on a regular basis. My friend was told not to return until she had lost a little more weight. I worked there until I was invited to my first afterparty with a black only crowd. I was nervous and didn't think they would like me because I had stretch marks on my body from giving birth and my boobs were small and my butt was kind of flat. Once I got on that stage and took my clothes off, the black guys went crazy! They loved me! I made so much money that night that I never went back to the white bars ever again.

The bars were okay, but I eventually wanted more and more money. I noticed that the bars had rooms in the back that the clients rented for fifteen dollars. The rooms had a bed and were only available for fifteen minutes at a time and nonrefundable. The clients would pay the dancers to have sex in these rooms. I began tricking, a.k.a. Prostitution, in the bars in those back rooms. Ashamed to say, I would charge the guys one hundred and fifty dollars for fifteen minutes of protected sex. Sometimes more, depending on the crowd.

The bars were restricted in ways that made most of the girls start having their own private after-hours parties in their own homes and other remote locations. The clients would rent facilities as well and have after hour parties for the dancers. When the clients gave an after-hour party, they would pay the dancers seventy-five to one hundred and fifty dollars to show up to these parties. Once you were paid to show up at the parties, you were required to dance at least an hour before you could leave with your payment.

They also had rooms for rent inside of these parties where the prostitution would take place. Of course, some would leave and go to hotels or even back to their homes to save money. I found myself doing more tricking than dancing. I was not a good dancer at all. I would just move very slowly, and seductively touching myself in a way that would catch the client's attention. Most of my money was made prostituting and putting on really freaky shows with pool table balls, fruit, and baby oil.

Although I hate to admit it, I did enjoy a lot of the parties and loved making that fast money. I got so money hungry that, at one point, I started making my own specials. My specials were a combination of twofers and threefers. Meaning I would have protected sex with a guy and his friend for a special price. I decided each and every night before

I went out how much money I needed that day. I wouldn't come home until I made that amount of money.

After a year or so, I began having flashbacks from the rapes I endured in my early teenage years. When the guys would touch me, I would get this burning feeling on my skin that reminded me of those guys. I slowly began to not like dancing and tricking anymore. But by that time, I had many regulars. Regulars were the guys that called and came back over and over at least three times a week.

With about four or five regulars a week, I was able to pay the bills and eventually stopped going to the after-hour parties. Things slowed down more and more over the months thereafter and I finally started looking for ways to deal with the pain I had buried way deep down inside my heart. I needed more out of my life and wanted more for myself and my children.

Meanwhile, I was still writing Trent and visiting him in prison. On a bus ride to the prison, I met a young lady named Tanisha Patty a. k. a. (Ne-Ne). R.I.P. Best friend/Sista! Tanisha was visiting her child's father at the time, and he was also doing a nine to twenty bit. We became very close friends during those long rides back and forth to the prison. I would ask her opinions about Trent's proposals to marry in prison. Her baby daddy wanted to marry her as well, but she insisted that they wait until he was released.

Ne-Ne and I took turns driving our cars and car-pooling other women who needed rides to the prison. I can remember one time we wanted to go on the bus to the prison and they were completely full that weekend. We wanted to go so bad that we agreed to a reduced fee to ride in the back hatch of the bus. We laughed all the way there because we looked crazy as hell balled up in the trunk squeezing together for about 9 hours to Kincheloe, MI. I think we visited them two-to-three times a month for years.

Chapter Six

THE PRISON WEDDING

Isaiah 40:31 KJV

"But they that wait upon the LORD shall renew their strength; they shall mount up with wings as eagles; they shall run, and not be weary; and they shall walk, and not faint."

It had been about two to three years that Trent had been in prison. I had been writing and visiting him every chance I could in my free time. Trent would write me asking that I read these bible verses and later discuss the verses with me to see if I had read them. He helped me find myself again through scriptures, which enabled me to quit prostituting and start looking for a brighter future. We got closer and closer through the letter writing back and forth and frequent visits to the penitentiary.

Trent's father had passed away and left him some money in the third year of his incarceration. I was on a visit, trying to console him because he wasn't able to attend his dad's funeral. All of a sudden, Trent got down on one knee in the prison visiting room and asked to me to marry him. He proposed to me. I was in shock. I can remember feeling so embarrassed but happy and surprised at the same time. I was

thinking to myself: I can't marry a man in prison with a nine-to-twenty-year sentence. My family would laugh me out so bad I could hear them already in my head.

I told him yes, but I really wanted to wait until he was released from prison. I asked that we at least wait out half of his time and then get married. So, at the end of the fourth year of incarceration, we got married in prison on June 27, 1995. Trent was struggling really bad with being in prison at this time, and I really wanted to help him make it through. Although I didn't want to get married in prison, I knew that I loved him and wanted to marry him one day anyway.

Getting married in prison was also my way of giving him hope to survive the next three to four years until his release date. A week before the wedding, I found out that I was pregnant. I had

no clue when it happened or whose it was. All I knew was, I had to get rid of it immediately! Sadly, it would be my sixth abortion, scheduled one day before my wedding. I should've known then that I was getting ready to make one of the biggest mistakes of my life!

I stood there, preparing to repeat my vow and bleeding so heavy I thought I would faint. As I was repeating the vow the chaplain had told me to repeat, for some reason, I blanked out and did not hear a word the chaplain said for a moment, and tried to mumble the words I thought I heard. I will never forget the look in Trent's eyes when he noticed I mumbled the words and didn't hear what he said. I knew right then that I was not supposed to be marrying this man or something like that. After the wedding, we had to leave and wait till the visiting hours to begin.

It was about an hour, so his mom, sister, and I went to go get food. When we returned, we stayed with him in the visiting room for the entire visit and took lots of pictures. At the end of the visit, we held each other so tight and wanted to jump into each other's pants, but, of course, we didn't have conjugal permission. The moment I arrived back home, there was more drama waiting for me.

BETRAYALS

Chapter Seven

THREE'S A CROWD

1 Corinthians 7:2-4 KJV

"Nevertheless, to avoid fornication, let every man have his own wife, and let every woman have her own husband. Let the husband render unto the wife due benevolence: and likewise, also the wife unto the husband. The wife hath not power of her own body, but the husband: and likewise, also the husband hath not power of his own body, but the wife."

After slowing down with all the partying, I began to prepare and look forward to my wedding day. It was two weeks before the wedding that I met this guy that made me a proposition I couldn't resist. I was walking down Grand River Road to the corner liquor store, with two of my friends. A car whipped around and parked along the street where we were walking, and a man got out of his vehicle and approached me and my friends. He stated his name and started to flirt with me, saying how he loved my summer dress. I thanked him and said I was married but he was welcome to any one of my friends.

I'll never forget what he said. "If I could have you for only two weeks, I'll take it." I wondered if he was serious. At the time, I was living in a drug-infested apartment building, struggling, and waiting for my prison wedding scheduled to happen within the next two weeks. He offered to buy all of our things in the store and followed us back to the apartment. We all talked with him, and as we drank and smoked his weed, I told him that we could be friends but I was married and could not do anything more with him.

His name was Noel, and he lived about fifteen minutes away in a much better neighborhood. Every day, he would call and ask me if I needed anything and would bring me whatever I wanted. I can remember going on the first date with him. He took me to the local mall and bought me an outfit from head to toe and paid to get my hair and nails done for the date. He made sure I felt good and looked good every day from the time I met him. Although I was getting married in two weeks, I told him I was already married to keep him from trying to talk me out of it like everyone else did.

Noel continued to come by every day after work and buy me everything I needed, and my friends, too. My fiancé's sister was so money hungry that she begged me to keep him on the side and take his money. She said that if I split the money with her, she wouldn't tell her brother in prison. Noel took me to many upscale restaurants, plays, and even out of the state a few times. However, two weeks later, the day of my prison wedding, I returned home to my drug infested apartment and my front door was wide open and hanging off the hinges and all my belongings were stolen from my apartment.

I was devastated and afraid to sleep in the apartment after that, and the manager of the building was nowhere to be found especially on the weekends. My new husband's sister had just pulled away after I entered the building and was on her way home for the night. Immediately, I called Noel and told him what had happened and asked if he could fix my door so that I could sleep there safely. Noel came over immediately, even though it was around three in the morning. He was unable to fix the door and suggested that I stay at his apartment in Dearborn Heights for the night until my apartment door was repaired.

I was so distraught I was not thinking that I just got married and I should not be sleeping at another man's home on my wedding night. Moreover, I ended up gathering some things and left with him because I was afraid to stay there and I thought it was too early in the morning to call someone to go to their house. Noel and I stayed up all morning, talking, and eventually had sex. He woke me out of my sleep; I didn't realize what I had done till after Noel went to work. I felt awful that I had sex with him. I completely forgot that it was my wedding night, so I had actually consummated my marriage with another man.

After Noel came home from work, he took me back to my apartment and we tried to find the manager to get the door replaced. When we arrived, there were drug addicts standing in the hallways, trash and debris all over the floors inside and outside the building, and

I did not feel safe there anymore. Eventually, I ended up staying at Noel's apartment, and that was when he offered me his proposition. He asked if he could take care of me, my son, and my husband in prison until my husband was released. He stated that my husband was not an issue for him at all because he actually had me in real life.

I thought that was rather cocky and strong of him to say, but, hey, he also allowed me to drive his car to and from the prisons to visit my husband. He made sure I had a new outfit to wear on the visits and lots of coins for pictures and the vending machines in the visiting room. I agreed to this arrangement and living with Noel, but my family was skeptical and advised me to leave immediately before things turned fatal. I was constantly reminding Noel that I loved my husband and that I would be getting my own home for my husband to come to before he was released from prison. Meanwhile, Noel continued to spoil me continuously with gifts and trips to places I'd never been before. There were only a few things about Noel that I didn't like.

For instance, Noel was a grease monkey and his hands and fingernails were so dirty, I hated for him to touch me. He also had an odor and said he was allergic to deodorant. This made me so uncomfortable with him that I only had sex with him maybe once every three to four months as payment for all the extravagant gifts and a free place to live. After a few years, Noel became more and more controlling and it began to scare me. He would take out his rifle and place it in a different corner of the house daily as a veiled threat.

I began to get a weird feeling about leaving when my husband came home. So, I began looking for a place to live and trying to save money for it. I didn't want Noel to know where I was moving to. I just wanted Trent to feel safe when he finally came home to me.

So, I immediately applied for an apartment about 30 minutes away and began saving every dime Noel gave me to buy stuff for the apartment.

It was early 2002 when I got busted by Noel for having the apartment. Noel came home from work early and retrieved the mail from the mailbox. It was a letter for me from the apartment complex with the rent receipt enclosed. Noel opened the mail and immediately asked what it was about. I told him the truth, and that following weekend, I actually moved into the apartment and thought I left Noel for good.

He was hurt and pissed when he found out that I was using his money for the last six months to pay the rent for an apartment. Then later, took me to court to try and take my son from me. (My next book will fascinate you even more when you read the baby daddy drama trauma). After a few months of fighting in court over our child together, I eventually allowed my son to live with his dad after all. Noel and I agreed to joint legal custody, while Noel had physical custody. I guess three's a crowd after all.

Chapter Eight

THE ONE-NIGHT-STAND FROM HELL

Romans 3:23KJV

"For all have sinned, and come short of the glory of God."

After finally moving out of Noel's house and into my own home, I started a job at a doctor's office where one of my childhood friends worked. It was at this doctor's office where I met my second baby daddy. He came into the office to be seen and three days later, began calling me at the office, saying he was my secret admirer. He would send flowers and lunches to my job anonymously. After about three weeks of these secret admirer shenanigans, my friend and I finally figured out who he was.

His name was Theodis, and he was a neighborhood dope dealer with thirteen kids and twelve baby mommas. My friend and I laughed and joked about how he had played this game with me because he knew I would not have been interested. But, for some strange reason, I still wanted to see him as a friend. He continued buying me lunch every day and giving me rides back and forth to work. I was trying to get a break from Noel because he was getting too possessive with me. It had been at least three months since I moved out of Noel's house, and, eventually, I invited Theodis over in an attempt at getting free weed from him.

After so many free lunches, free weed, and free rides to work, I eventually tried to have protected sex with him. I was lonely and horny, waiting for my husband to be released from prison. During our first sexual encounter, Theodis stopped in the beginning of my orgasm and stated, "I can't feel anything. Can we take the condom off?" I can remember being so frustrated that he messed up my orgasm like that. I wanted to complete the orgasm, so I agreed and told him to hurry up and be careful not to leak inside me.

Three to four weeks later, I was at work at the doctor's office and began vomiting. My friend and I did a blood pregnancy test at the office and it came back positive. I was devastated! I

told Theodis, and he was pissed. He came up to the doctor's office, demanding that I come outside. He stated that he didn't want any more kids and wanted to help me abort the baby the old-fashioned way with a hanger.

I was terrified because I could see in his eyes, he was serious. He became loud and belligerent at my job to the point that the doctor had to call the police to have him removed from the premises. I began to understand why it was so dangerous to date a dope dealer. By this time, it was my first-year wedding anniversary and I was trying to make plans to go visit my husband at the prison. Of course, I wanted an abortion because I didn't want my husband to find out that I was pregnant by another man.

Although I had planned to have the abortion, the night before my scheduled appointment, I had a terrifying dream. My dream had reminded me that I'd already had six abortions and I only had one child at the time. Which meant that this one would be my seventh abortion. I felt like God was reminding me that the number seven was an important number. I woke up, afraid of what side effects the abortion could have, knowing I only had one child and wanted to have a little girl later with my husband.

I thought that if I had a seventh abortion, I would die or something would happen to me medically and I wouldn't be able to get pregnant again. Eventually, I decided to keep the baby, and a couple months later, Theodis attacked me. I will never forget that night. It was about eleven at night when he knocked on the door. I was about six months pregnant with his child and laying on a pallet I made on the floor in my living room.

Theodis was still selling drugs on the corner of my block and would come over to use the bathroom and/or pay me to hold things for him. After the knock at the door, I opened it and immediately walked back into the living room to lay back down. I listened for him to lock my door when he left. About fifteen minutes later, I noticed that I never heard him leave and I got up to make sure my door was locked.

As I walked into the kitchen towards the backdoor, I saw a woman leaning on the kitchen counter. Theodis was sitting on my kitchen counter with his head laid back into the upper cabinet. The woman was giving him oral sex. I watched for a second, but didn't say a word as I reached for the backdoor knob and opened it. Theodis and the lady heard the door open and the lady stopped and ran outside.

Theodis was drunk and irate. "Close the damn door. And why you staring at me like that?" I didn't say anything. I just continued to hold the door open, hoping he would walk out and leave me alone. He jumped down off the counter and slammed the door shut. I walked back into the living room, and he followed me, saying he was sorry. I refused to speak and just kept turning my back to him, pretending not to hear him at all.

As I sat down on the chair in the living room, rubbing my belly and looking down at the floor, I felt something hit me in the back of my head. I looked up, and he had hit me with his fist so hard in the back of my head that water came out of my eyes. I thought my eyeballs were bleeding. I jumped up and tried to run away from him, and he chased me around the house. I ran around my dining room table until he flipped it over and glass shattered everywhere.

He then grabbed me by the back of my hair and forced my head through the dining room glass window and it shattered on the back of my neck. I was so scared. I just knew my unborn baby would not survive this. I fell on the floor and balled my body up in the fetal position, trying to protect my large belly. He held his foot over my belly, saying, "Get up now or I will stomp that baby out of you." I begged him to stop.

He picked me up off the floor and walked over to the balcony and threatened to toss me over the side if I didn't look at him.

Hesitantly, I walked over to the chair and sat down. He began to cry, begging me to call the police on him and handed me the phone. I was even more afraid to call the police. He said that he was out on parole and that if I called the police, he would have to do the remaining time on his previous offense. While my eye was swollen shut, I just sat there and listened to him explaining how sorry he was and he didn't mean to hurt me like that. He thought I was acting high and mighty like he was nothing and it made him angry to be ignored. Moreover, he felt that it would have to be worth it to spend the rest of his life in prison.

Theodis was so ashamed and afraid for anyone to see my eye that he actually stayed at my house and held me hostage for about three weeks until my eye was completely healed. I was not allowed to go outside or answer my home phone. He ran all my errands and told my friends and family that I was at the doctors or in the shower when they called or stopped by. After my eye was no longer a disgrace, being six months pregnant and all, I was finally able to get out and mingle again with neighbors and friends.

I was afraid to tell my family because he threatened to kill my mom or anyone whom I talked to. Because he was this big-time dope dealer, I believed him. It was my first and last time dating a street thug. After about a month of that, I finally called Noel and told him what I had been through with Theodis. Noel, afraid for my life, came and packed my things while Theotis was away and moved me into a friend's house on the other side of town. There, I then gave birth to my second child while looking for a new home for me and my two children.

Chapter Nine

THE DIVORCE

Matthew 19:6 KJV

"So, they are no longer two, but one flesh. Therefore, what God has joined together, let no one separate."

I will never forget the day I arrived at the prison on our first wedding anniversary. My hair was done, my outfit was cute, and I was so excited to see my first love, my beautiful husband. After going through the security process, I waited patiently for the guards to bring my husband down to the visiting room. He walked over to me and we held each other and smiled. When we sat down at the table, he said, "I need to ask you a question. Please don't lie to me. If you really love me, you will tell me the truth. But if you lie, I will hate you forever."

I looked at him, thinking, I love you more than anything and I will never lie to you. I always believed that the truth would set you free. My husband looked me in the eyes and asked, "Are you cheating on me? Yes or no?" Immediately, my eyes started to tear up, and he called the guard and asked to be taken back to his cell. I tried to stop him and explain, but he was not trying to hear anything I had to say. I was just sitting there in shock.

I was escorted back to the lobby of the prison. I sat there for about two hours then asked the guards to go and ask him to come back out to the visiting room. The guards went and asked him, but he refused to come back out. However, I sat another two hours and asked the guards again to go and ask him if he would please come back down to talk to me. Again, he refused. The visiting hours were until eight that evening, and I stayed there the entire time, begging the guards to tell him this and to tell him that. But he refused every time and left me there sitting in the lobby, crying my eyes out until the prison closed. I finally got into my car to drive about eight hours back home.

I continuously wrote letters and every one of them was returned back to me unopened. After about two years of begging for another chance and ignoring all divorce filings, I remember the one statement made by him that finally made me sign the divorce papers. Trent wrote to me in a letter, "Why would you want to stay married to someone who doesn't want to be with you?" In that moment, I begin to feel embarrassed to be holding a man hostage against his will.

A man, in prison, from a crack addiction, and serving 9 to 20? I had to be out of my mind to be fighting to keep a person with a history like that. I always felt that if I would be with a man with a horrible past and status like prison, it would be because that man loved me unconditionally and would not let me leave him alone, not the other way around. I also felt that he should've been grateful that any woman would marry a man that had a drug addiction and was capable of tying up an old lady to her wheelchair to rob her. So, if he wanted out that bad, I'd better run while I could, period! Although I felt all these things, I still wanted to fight the divorce until he was released and able to give our marriage a real try.

During the divorce hearing, the Judge noticed that I was pregnant and asked Trent if he was the father. I know Trent will never forget that moment! Again, I was pregnant by the one-night stand from hell and I decided that I was not going to kill an innocent baby for a man that didn't even want me. I had six abortions before in the past and was not willing to have a seventh abortion to save a marriage that was already in the process of ending. My God has shown me previously in a dream that I would die if I had aborted a seventh baby. I was afraid to die as well during the procedure.

The fact that my husband would divorce me without even giving me a second chance or a chance to even explain, was the reason why I did not regret being pregnant at the divorce proceedings. It seemed to be a right on time payback for a man that married me for the wrong reasons and was willing to leave me at the drop of a hat with no conversation, forgiveness, or nothing! It was a right on time revenge I never even meant or planned. Unfortunately, it wasn't that simple for me to move on after the divorce. But I did learn that I can do all things through Christ Jesus, which strengthens me.

Trent was released eventually and immediately married another woman in Texas where he was paroled and still is today. Unfortunately, I never saw or heard from him, my first and only true love, ever again. It was years later I found out that Noel actually wrote my husband in prison after I left him and said God knows what! To this day, I still don't know what was written in that letter and I suppose I never will. The end result was I decided to build a closer relationship with God, Noel married his high school sweetheart, and I didn't hear from Trent again.

Chapter Ten

ALMOST FAMOUS

Joshua 23:6 6 KJV

"Be very strong; be careful to obey all that is written in the Book of the Law of Moses, without turning aside to the right or to the left."

I love to sing, and when I was just about 10, I can remember my mom used to take me for singing lessons every Wednesday afternoon afterschool in the Wayne State University campus area. Whitney Houston was my favorite female artist, and singing her songs everyday was how I trained and developed my voice. After years of just randomly singing for people and strangers everywhere, I finally got the courage up to audition in front of millions! It was between 2000 and 2002, right here in the City of Detroit. It was for one of P Diddy's "talent searches". I heard about it through friends and they really wanted me to go an audition.

I decided to go to my very first audition! P Diddy was not there; I believe his people were handling everything. I sung one of my favorite's songs by Faith Evans, "Soon as I Get Home". That was the very moment I knew I could sing! I was a starving artist that day, waiting in line outside of the Fox Theatre. It had been a line stretched for miles and I got in that line one whole day before the auditions even began with my blanket and pillow.

The moment I stepped on that stage; I could hear my singing instructors voice reminding me to project my voice to the clouds. I envisioned singing to my ex-husband all the way on the other side of the earth and my voice ranged the entire building. There were about four to five people in the audience, doing the judging, and they began to huddle in a circle. I was then called down to the judges and told to sit with them while they discussed some things. There was ten minutes of wondering, What the hell? Did I just make it? I was very excited! Then one of them approached me and asked for my phone number and stated that I would be called if needed.

I can remember running out the door, jumping, kicking, and screaming!! They loved me! They didn't know what to do with me, though. I felt that was only because of my age. They were only looking for people under 25 at that time, but I was reassured that day that I could sing and I could be a celebrity if I wanted. Although I never did hear back from them, their reactions alone were all I needed to believe I was good enough to make my own album!

Not long after that experience, I was watching television and I saw a commercial come on in big letters, "TALENT SEARCH". At the time, I was living with Noel and my three sons. The commercial said that they were coming to Detroit and having open auditions for all interested. Actors and singers were wanted by over 100 major industry label companies. They were holding open call auditions in a Downtown Detroit Hotel Conference room. If anyone receives a call back card from the judges, they would be invited to spend two entire days with over 100 Top Record and Commercial Label companies in the City of Chicago at The Navy Pier. Everyone would have a chance to audition one by one in hopes of obtaining another call back card from the labels to discuss a possible signing deal afterward. I got so excited!

I spoke to Noel and my other children's fathers about the opportunity. Everyone insisted that I should go and were even willing to keep the kids. I was sure I could win a record deal and promised all three of my children's fathers that if they kept their kid while I auditioned. I would buy them all houses if I made it big. I really believed that I could possibly land 1 call back card out of 100. The kids' dads made me sign or do certain things to help them provide for the kids while I was gone. It was understandable and of course I wanted my kids to have access to anything they may have needed if I was away for long.

I was going to try my best to make it in Chicago for my kids. When I arrived at the first auditions in Detroit, I was given some commercial scripts on small little pieces of paper. It was like short commercial ads with only about 3 to 4 lines. My commercial script was a Burger King advertisement. It said something along the lines of, "I love my big burger. I can have lettuce, tomatoes, pickles, onions, and sauce on my big burger and have my bun toasted just the way I like it. Burger King is my favorite burger place!" However, I had so much energy when I said my script, I even jumped up on the judge's desk and smiled really big at the end about My Big Burger! They loved me and thought I was funny and then invited me to Chicago's Navy Pier National Auditions.

Once Noel and the other dads saw that I made it to the finals, everyone was willing to help me get there and prepare for it. However, a couple days before I left to the final auditions in Chicago, all hell broke loose! I was looking in the garage for something. I forget what it was. When I stumbled across an opened strange and unknown box, I saw a smaller box inside. I began to open the small box and there was a stack of beautiful wedding invitations.

They were individually wrapped in these soft tissues and small ribbons holding the little cards inside. As I untied the ribbons and unfolded the card, it read...On this day, blah blah blah we are joining together Noel and who? Oh yes hunty! Noel was scheduled to be married in a couple of weeks! To another woman? Mind you, I had just had his baby about six months prior. I was furious! Marriage? Right under my nose? I immediately began to put a plan in action to destroy this wedding and Noel altogether! My first real baby mama drama!

Noel worked the midnight shift at a local plant at the time. I decided I would get dropped off to his job and steal his car. I had a friend drop me off at his job at two-three o'clock in the morning. I jumped into his van started the car and pulled off! I can remember I couldn't even wait to get home. I drove only a few blocks and pulled over so that I could go through all his belongings he had in the van.

He left his phone and his wallet in the car and I thought to myself… Let the games began! I started listening to his voicemails first. I heard messages from the wedding planner and the venue manager. I began returning the calls, as his fiancée, and began canceling all their reservations one by one! You can't even imagine the laughter I had while I did this. I was thinking, I got these m'f'ers! I mean, I cancelled everything!

I even changed his voicemail message on his cell phone to let others know how I was running stuff! The voice message said something like, "Hello, you've reached Mr. & Mrs. Noel! Please leave him or I a message and we will get back to you as soon as possible." I'm sure it was a little more dramatized than I can recall from thirty years ago. But after I changed as much as I could on his phone and in his wallet, I took the van home and made him fetch a ride home that day.

He had no clue about the wedding cancellations, but he did know about his phone voicemail. I can remember he came home mad, asking that I give him his password to change his voicemail back. I laughed, and after a few hours of arguing about it, I eventually gave him the password to get into his own voicemail.

The next day was my audition! I already had my bus ticket and planned to go without telling Noel. Everything was all set, and I had gotten dropped off at the bus station early so that I could check-in and hide until my bus left. After the check-in, I went to the bathroom and as I was coming out, guess who I saw?

Man, oh man, I was shaking like booty meat! I was hiding behind walls and plants just like in the movies. Once I saw my escape plan to the bus loading area, I whispered softly to the bus driver. "Please sir. Can you please let me on this bus now? There's a man in the bus terminal lobby looking for me and he's going to kill me!" I pointed to Noel, and the driver told me to hurry and sit low!

He said, "I will not let him on this bus, I promise you."

I hurried to the back of the bus and sunk down in the seat as I watched Noel pace from the bus loading area to the check-in counter. He was waiting for me with vengeance in his eyes, baby. We had about 20 minutes till take off, but it seemed like 2 hours in that moment! After about ten minutes of me hiding on the bus, Noel approached the bus driver. He asked about me and if he could look on the bus quickly.

I could hear the bus driver stating that he couldn't let him board without a ticket. He also stated to Noel that he had too many personal items of passengers on the bus and could not allow him to search the bus and assured him that I had not loaded on the bus as of yet. As the bus slowly pulled off, I sat up in the window and put my thumbs in my ears and stuck my tongue out at Noel looking up at the bus windows. I laughed all the way to Chicago while thinking of how I got his ass back! He called repeatedly, causing me to turn the ringer off.

Once I arrived at the hotel and unpacked my things, I was so excited to be in Chicago and started preparing for the long walk across to the Navy Pier. The Navy Pier was filled with the top modeling, acting and music label company scouters from all over the world. Remember I made the finalists with the Burger King Commercial audition not the music! Saturday morning, I began auditioning with the commercial scripts they had prepared for us to use during the interviews.

At around my tenth interview with still no call back cards for acting or commercials, I began to walk around the place to see how things were looking for others. As I walked into the hallway on the opposite side, I began to hear singing. I followed the voices to just the other side of the wall. There were over 50 top record label companies interviewing singers and band groups. I immediately noticed that there was a different color wrist band for that particular area and you would have to have a wrist bracelet to enter the interview floor. My mind was racing, trying to figure out how to get in that room and sing my heart out. Singing is my passion and I really wanted to be over there on that side instead of the modeling and acting side.

After being told that I was only granted permission to the acting and modeling interviews, I decided that I would sing from the hallway. I started to sing the song by Faith Evans, "Soon as I Get Home" at the top of my lungs, hoping that someone would hear me. The moment I hit that high note part, "I get down on my knees, begging you please, I'm so Sorry!" It seemed like the whole room got quiet and everyone was looking at me! A man came to me and asked me to come in the room.

After I crossed that threshold, they were fighting over me just a bit. I was told, "Don't sing another note!" "Stay right next to me; don't take anymore cards." It was the exact response I thought they would have when they heard me sing! I just knew I would be famous sooner or later. By the end of the night, I had about five or six call back cards from record labels and an invite to Florida for an in-person interview due to me not having a demo prepared.

When I got back to my room, I was trying to figure out a way to fly to Florida with some of the producers I met. This weekend trip was completely exhausting and all I had left was my luggage filled with dirty clothes and my ticket back to Michigan. My phone was out of minutes and all my money was spent. There was no way I could leave for Florida with strangers I just met, and I didn't even have money for a phone call. It was also clear to me that my children had to be at school the next morning and I had to be home for my kids.

So, I decided to just go home and work on my demo since I knew now that the music industry would love me!

GROWING PAINS

Chapter Eleven

THE TURNAROUND

Romans 8:28 KJV

"And we know that all things work together for good to them that love God, to them who are the called according to his purpose."

I was at the Motor City Casino and saw a guy whom I met through an ex, named Robby. He often spoke up when he saw me, but this time we chatted for a minute about his cousin and he stated that he wanted to give him my number later that day when he saw him. Well, he eventually called me and we met up at his mom's house one day. He was telling me about how he was managing a few artists and trying to start his own record label company. Robby knew I loved to sing, and we talked about making music together in the past.

I had recently left Noel again and had been in my own apartment at the time for only a few months. Soon, Robby and I began riding back and forth to the studio, looking for beats to start creating my first album. The studio was located in Pontiac, MI about 45 minutes from Inkster, where I was living at the time. The drive was so long and the nights became so late that Robby asked me if I wanted to move to

Pontiac, MI so I could be closer to the studio. He then brought me an application, I filled it out, and returned it to the Pontiac Apartment Office the following week.

I was approved for the new apartment in Pontiac very quickly and moved-in within a month or so. Once I moved to Pontiac, Robby managed to get me a few beats and I wrote a couple songs to them and eventually ended up writing my first 10 track album. Robby had moved me in an apartment right down the street from his house. Unfortunately, Robby and I were creeping and cheating, doing the Ike and Tina in the studio, and my music ended up left by the wayside. Robby eventually disappeared and left me in Pontiac to fend for myself.

I had only recorded one of my songs. Soon after his disappearance, I got a call from my sister that my dad died. Coincidently, she was standing with my aunt at the dollar store, when our aunt received a call from my uncle, saying, "Get over here now! Willie's dead!"

When my aunt and sister arrived at my dad's apartment, my aunt asked, "Who is coming to get the body"?

He said nobody and that the police came and pronounced him dead and stated that they see this all the time and left. My uncle said the paramedics noticed the blood coming from his legs along with the abscesses and just left him sitting there inside the shared apartment on the couch. People from his building were going in and out, looking and staring the whole time. My aunt eventually got a hold of a funeral home director and scheduled for my dad's body to be picked up. Because rigor mortis had set in and my dad was stuck in a sitting position, the funeral home ended up dropping him down the stairs on the way out. My dad's face was bruised by the fall and it was visible at the viewing.

Willie a.k.a. "Cadre" a.k.a. "capper" a.k.a. "Tido" Edward "White" Wilson, had a history of being a slick street hustler with the side nicknames to match. He was the oldest of twenty-two children. Because of his expensive drug habit, my grandma would call me every time she knew of my dad getting a check, so that I got some of it before he spent it all. My grandma would call me every time she knew of my dad getting a check. She'd tell me, "Baby, hurry up and get here. The mail's about to run and your daddy got a check on the way."

I'd get there so fast even before the mail lady sometimes. She was so quick with it, I missed her. My dad would always say, "Mama why you got my baby here like this?

And she'd say, "To get some of that money you got coming."

He'd laugh and say, "Okay. The check isn't much but I will give you what I can." I would always take more than he was willing to chuck over. He spoiled me rotten and told me that if any man looked into my eyes longer than five minutes, he would listen to my story.

My dad was a very known brother in the hood and feared by many. He also was a pimp, and a heavy drug user since the age of ten. He was in prison when I was conceived. Although he wasn't the typical father, he was my hero, he loved me, and I loved him with all my heart.

When I was little, my mom used to send me to be with him during the summer.

Oh boy did I love going to my dad's house and to my grandmas too. My dad used to take me to hustle with him. He always said, "You want to eat? Then let's go to work." At the age of about eight, I would drive around the parking lot of the business office suites, while my dad hung out the back door stealing hubcaps from off the tires of the cars in the parking lot. I was so short; I couldn't even see the road or where I was going.

I was so scared, but I wanted my dad to get the money so that we could have a good breakfast and stay in to watch some TV. One day, I remember I was driving really close to a car so my dad could get the hubcaps off and the owner of the vehicle walked up. I almost pooped my pants for real that day. The man started to chase us as my dad was hanging out the back door, yelling, "Pull off!" I tried but I couldn't see over the wheel and I didn't know how to drive.

The man grabbed my dad out of the car and they tussled for a few seconds as I was rolling through the parking lot. He yelled, "Go! My dad wanted me to drive faster and he was going to jump back in the car as I was moving. Like some Dukes of Hazard type stuff. I thought I was going to leave him, but he did jump back in the car and I pushed it to the corner so that he could jump in and get away. To this day, I can't believe some on the things my dad and I had done together.

Another time, some people had owed my dad money. I can remember him giving me a gas can and we both poured it around the window seals until they came out of the house. We were going to set that house on fire, but the man begged and my dad gave him another chance. It took me a long time to understand what my dad was really up to. We walked the streets a lot when I stayed with him for the summers.

There used to be sheltered benches for sitting at the bus stops all up and down Woodward Ave. People would be packed in there in the winter months to keep warm. My dad and I would wake up early and sit in those bus shelters talking to any and everybody for hours, while we waited for whatever he was planning for that day. Some of them would go home with us and then disappear in my dad's room for a while. One day, the door was cracked, and I saw my dad helping her with a long rubber cord, wrapping it around her forearm. I knew then that he was shooting her up with drugs, but what I didn't know was if it was consensual or not.

The girls would always leave his room in a different state from when they first came. The conversations at the bus stop would always start off like, "Hey, that's your daughter. She's cute?" I think I heard him tell one girl that I was on my way to school and needed my hair combed. I believe that was how he'd get these young girls and women to leave with him. But then again, my dad was so slick, my grandma said he could sell you your panties while they were still on you.

Unconditional: The Innocence, Betrayals, and Growing Pains

Like I said earlier, it took years for me to understand what my dad was really doing when he brought girls home. I'm still a bit confused, but I know he used me a few times to meet girls at the bus stops, took them home, drugged them up, and then said they owed him money. He would then drop them off where they could make his money. It's still a hard thing to imagine or even articulate. Because my dad was everything to me and he was my hero.

I've heard some awful stories about my dad and I know he's done most of them. Strangely enough, I can't seem to connect the disgust of it all. My daddy was so feared and well known that people knew me as lil Tido. When I entered a room, people seemed to be extra nice to me and tried to suck up to me so that my dad would not come after them. He even allowed me to throw a woman out of his apartment one day just because I said I didn't like her.

My dad had another daughter before me, though he was not sure if she was his. Me being a jealous and only daughter, I made him swear that he would never have or claim another child besides me. I told him I wanted to be the only child and he made me think I was until my sister found me many years later. He was my hero. I love you, Daddy. Willie Edward Wilson September 25, 1947 – June 25, 2005.

When it was time to bury my dad, it seemed like everyone who hated him came out of nowhere. They rejoiced and apologized to me at the same time, saying how awful he was to them. We had no money and no way to bury our daddy so I called on my aunt, his baby sister,

Aunt Resa. She emailed folks and posted on Facebook until the cremation was almost paid in full. Aunty took her brother's funeral needs to the nation for help. My aunty got that money up to bury her brother, my daddy. Thank You. Lord Father God.

He sat in the funeral freezer for about three months before he was cremated, and we never paid the remaining balance for the death certificate. Later on, depression gave me a need for isolation. I became so withdrawn I became distant with everyone. I really just needed to know my purpose. By this time, all my children were still with their dads for summer break and in the process of coming back home to live in Pontiac, MI.

The struggle was real those first few months there all by myself, trying to survive in Pontiac. I ended up linking up with one of Robby's friends named, T-Bone. T-Bone was into credit card fraud and identity theft. He saw how broke I was and asked if I wanted to make some money. He said, "All you have to do is drive and I will buy your food and give you money for gas."

I drove him and his friend around town from store to store while they ran all the credit cards they had. I was so tired that day, so I told him that I was staying in the van and wasn't going in any stores. All I can remember is some tapping on the van window that woke me up from my brief nap I was taking while T-Bone was in a store. When I opened my eyes, my van was completely surrounded with police and guns pointing directly at me! I heard, "Freeze! Don't move! Get out the vehicle now!" I started to reach for my purse, and they all begin shouting at me! "Freeze! Freeze!" I stopped instantly and held my hands up high so they could see them, as I was told. Once they snatched me from the van, I saw T-Bone getting escorted out of the store and his friend, too. I just shook my head and followed the instructions of the officers all the way to Rochester Hills, MI city jail.

It was so funny, though, because the officers were running my name in the system over and over again. It was so clean, one of the officers came to show me a blank report with my name at the top. He asked, "Young lady, why are you out here with them stealing?" I explained to him that I was hungry and needed food and gas for my vehicle. I told them I fell asleep waiting for them to return to the car and I didn't know what they were doing.

The officer asked a few questions about the guys I was with, and I sung like a canary! I was not going to jail in Rochester Hills. They eventually released me after I told everything I knew. As soon as they opened the gate, I saw the guys being released as well. I was worried they were going to get me for snitching.

However, we all ended up walking about ten miles back to Pontiac. It was the longest walk I had ever taken of my life. The police had taken my van and I couldn't get it back because it was in my baby daddy's name. He had a warrant, and was not going to the police impound with his license. My apartment in Pontiac was right across the way from a church that I had walked past several times, thinking one day I would enter. With all the depression I was feeling at the time, I was sure that if I didn't go back to church soon, I would be dead.

So, one day, still feeling very low in spirit, I decided to try God one last time. I felt like it was my last attempt to change my life for the better. I told God that I was tired of watching my kids hunger and be without the basic things in life. I felt that my mistakes would ultimately prevent me from ever being able to provide for my children. The statistics showed how many women like me would end up after 30 years, and I could see it happening already.

There I was, a single mother, three children, no job, on welfare, and without reliable transportation. Moreover, it was the typical coming from the average disconnected teenage girl living in the ghetto of the City of Detroit. The day I walked into that church across from my apartment, was the beginning of a major turnaround for me. There was a big conference going on with a guest speaker, named Mrs. J. Hadden. I was tired of the nonsense in churches and was bold enough to sit in the third row closest to the front.

Mrs. J. began telling her testimony and shouted out for God to show her the woman suffering from depression and to come forth now! I started to think of course, it was me? But quickly sat back to listen further. Joyce shouted. "You have been crying too long, my sister, and you don't believe God heard you! I want to ask you to give God a chance today."

She said, "Just come on up here right now and let me anoint your head and watch God show you who he is and how he has been waiting for you! I was the type of person that had my doubts but still wanted to believe. I was tired of folks lying on God and I knew I was not going to be doing no falling out on the floor and definitely not speaking in no "tongues" (spiritual language). So yeah, I got up, but just to prove her wrong! I walked up to the alter where she was standing.

She placed three dots of oil on my forehead and told me to walk to the other side of the altar, touch the wall, and then walk to the other side of the altar and touch the other wall. She said by the time I got back to center with her, God was going to change my mind today. In Jesus Name! The precious thing about this moment is that I always believed that speaking in tongues was a lie and that if God wanted to prove he was real to me, he would have to fill me with his holy spirit and make me speak in tongues as well.

Baby! By the time I made it back to the other side of the altar and met back in the center with Mrs. J., she touched my forehead again and then BAM!!! I whelped out like a trumpet and began speaking in tongues filled with the holy spirit like never before! I was speaking so profoundly that it actually sounded like another language, not just babbling. They laid me down on the floor and covered me halfway with a quilt. I just laid there and cried my eyes out to the lord.

It felt as though I was just telling him all that was wrong with me but in another language. My mind was playing a movie of my life, and I began to cry harder and harder. I believe I laid there on the floor at the center of the altar for the remainder of the service. I just didn't want to let go of the holy spirit flowing all through my mind, body, and soul.

On my way home to my apartment, I remember still speaking in tongues very softly. I wanted to savor the moment for as long as possible. I fell asleep that night still glorifying God and filled with his anointed healing power. My life changed drastically after that worship service. I began going to church every Sunday and any other service they would have there. I even came to clean and plant flowers whenever the church needed help doing that as well.

The pastor there was quite a man of God and he taught me how pray. I was a faithful member of that church for a very long time. However, after about six long years of living Holy before the Lord, I became very anxious for companionship. This was the longest I'd ever gone without sex and I was not aware of the lusting adrenaline that was building up inside of me. I believe I was under some type of spiritual attack and I began trying to figure out ways to be in the presence of men.

Let's just say after six years of abstinence, I was hotter than a firecracker! Things started to get different and I wanted some sex. I started having sexual dreams and couldn't seem to stop fantasizing about different men and different ways to have sex with them. There was a program opening at the community college for learning heating and cooling. At first, I thought, heck no, I'm not the heating and cooling type. I was offered a spot in the program several times until I realized that I would be the only woman in the class. So, I entertained the idea of joining a program with only men in order to meet someone I could eventually have sex with. I know. Crazy right? But yeah, I wanted to be queen of the jungle.

I sat in the front seat, front row of the classroom. After I sat there, I was pissed because I couldn't see all the men in the class without turning around. When I turn around, I saw this guy looking dead at me. It was like he was already waiting for my turnaround.

I thought to myself, "Who is that?" I needed to look at him one more time just to verify what I saw and felt the first time. When I turned around the second time, our eyes locked and I literally felt like I was naked and he could see me. My mind was racing. Why did it feel like that? I was really hot and bothered but a little afraid at the same time. During class, I noticed that he was cute; nerdy looking, clean cut, and smelled absolutely delicious.

On the third day, I was surely ready to make a move. Six years of no sex can take a toll on a woman in ways I never even imagined. So, during class attendance I got his name. Let's just call him Edouble. Edouble seemed to be a quiet guy, and he drove a large van with old writing on it from a neighborhood church. The cologne he wore made my body pulsate all over.

It had been a long time since I had ever felt this attracted to anyone, and it felt really good. Assuming it was a sign from heaven, I decided to shoot my shot. Edouble was walking to the bathroom and I was walking alongside him. As we approached the men's entrance, I asked, "Do you need some help with that?"

He turned and looked at me and said, "Sure." Immediately, we walked into the men's bathroom stall together and closed the door.

As he pulled down his pants and whipped it out, I reached for it. I held on till the very last drop, shook it off, and placed it back in his underwear. The stare I got from him was to die for. Later, we talked and he informed me that he had a girlfriend. The proposition then became clear. I was looking for some short-term fun and a chance to let off some steam.

We would periodically call each other for help on the homework assignments. One time, I went to his home. I will admit, I planned to screw him and I was not taking no for an answer. When I arrived at his home, he had a friend there. I was so nervous about how I was going to seduce this man, I decided to hit the weed they were smoking when I walked in. His friend was lingering too long and I knew the night was going to end soon, so I just sat on his leg while he was explaining the homework assignment to me.

The friend took heed and began his exit speech as he headed out the door. He even stated on his way out that he didn't want to interrupt anything. So, I think he got the picture and I appreciated that in that moment. Edouble stated to me that he was going to take a shower and then drop me off at home shortly after. It wasn't long before I was pregnant with my little girl.

My close and dear friend/Sista, Nakita Shenay Jamison, may she R.I.P., was the one that told me I was pregnant before I had even missed a period. Kita actually told me she had a dream I was going to have a baby girl long before I even got pregnant. I laughed because I hadn't had sex for almost six years at that time. We couldn't wait until the ultrasound. We were all excited to find out the gender of the baby. It was Kita, and my three boys all there with me at my doctor's appointment.

The moment the doctor showed us the baby was a girl, I started crying right there while lying on the table. My three boys hugged me, and we were all so happy. Kita told me, "Okay, now I'm her god-mother and I'm going to spoil her rotten because I knew her before she was even born." Kita was the best godmother ever, too. I can remember when my daughter was only about 2 or 3, Kita went and bought her a two-piece bikini! It was so funny because she really wanted my daughter to wear that swimsuit and I was not having it.

She would always buy my daughter stuff that was too grown or inappropriate for her, but she meant well.

Because there were only four school bus stops circling our apartment complex, my boys would have to stand in front of Kita's apartment. She would keep an eye out for them on the days I had to work early. Kita saved my babies a few times from the bus stop bullies and always called me immediately if she saw anything strange at the bus stop. When it rained, she would bring my kids inside her apartment and make them wait inside her door until the bus came. I was new to the neighborhood and Kita made sure I knew who everyone was and who not to talk to.

Kita had a rare condition where she was born with a hole in her heart. Her dad and her youngest daughter had died previously from it. She had two kids, a boy and a girl, that were about my boys' age, and they all played together a lot. She also needed a kidney and was on dialysis daily. I often went with her and kept her company for her 4-hour treatment.

She came from a large family, and they were well known, respected, and feared in the community. I loved her, and she was very protective over her friends and family. Whenever I'd mention her name to folks in the neighborhood, everyone would get quiet and start treating me even nicer. We met in a program where we were trying to find employment and been friends ever since. We lived in the same apartment complex across the parking lot from one another.

So, one day, she complained about her chest pains and decided to go to the hospital. When she woke up in another state, they told her she needed immediate surgery and they had to air lift her to an Ohio State Hospital for the procedure. Kita told me when she found out she was in Ohio, she started cussing and fussing at those doctors for taking her away from her kids without permission. She argued that her kids were to be released from school and were walking home.

They asked if someone could pick her kids up and she insisted that her kids were locked out of the house and she had to get home now. They then informed her that if she left, she may not make it next time to the hospital. Without further ado, after stabilizing her, Kita was released and bused back home as she demanded. She told them she would see about the surgery later. Kita also explained to me that she would die without a stint and she'd rather work on her kidney problem first. She thought one illness would kill her before the other and was willing to take her chances.

Almost one year later, the chest pains returned and she knew it was not good. She even called me and told me that she was having these chest pains and said she was thinking about going to the hospital if it didn't get better after a while. Not long after, while visiting at a cousin's house, I got a phone call stating that Kita had just arrived at the hospital and it didn't look good. Immediately, I called her phone, not thinking at all, and her daughter answered. It was one of the most painful moments in my life to hear a child watch her mother die.

She explained to me that her mom called her and ask if she would drive her to the hospital. She said she drove in the emergency bay and parked the car to jump out for a wheelchair. After getting the wheelchair, she proceeded to push her mom up to the emergency check-in window. The nurse then came from behind the desk and asked Kita if she could stand up. Kita nodded and stood straight up. The moment she stood up, her eyes rolled into the back of her head and she fell back into the wheelchair.

The nurses then rushed her to a room, started life saving procedures, and that was the very moment I called Kita's phone and her daughter answered. I was only planning on going to the viewing because Kita always told me to stay away from her family because they were too dangerous. But my boys were not having it. Thank God! And one of my sons, who was seventeen at the time, took three busses to meet me there. Because he was on the other side of town visiting with his dad. The funeral was packed for blocks with nowhere to park.

As I approached the funeral home, I noticed an empty spot right at the front door. It was so on time that I really felt like Kita or the Lord up above had saved that spot just for us. I miss you and I love you, Nakita Shenay Jamison! R.I.P. 06/08/1975-10/06/2013. After Kita's death, I had crying spelling for months until I eventually left my daughter's father for good and moved at least thirty minutes away. To make a long story short, the details and steps to my healing process will come in a series of books following this one so stay tuned.

But I can tell you this: it didn't stop there and it got worse before it got better. After a horrific long and drawn-out drama-filled ending with Edouble, I put all those negative things behind me and began to grow spiritually, emotionally, and mentally for myself, my sons, and my very own little princess. I ended up in a domestic violence homeless shelter, and again my next book will go into more details of the baby daddy syndrome I experienced while being a mother of four with four daddies. It was the domestic violence homeless shelter where my life's turnaround started to bear fruit. It was also a place I fought so hard not to end up in, especially not right after buying my first home.

I will never forget how I just wanted to cry myself to sleep after finishing all that paperwork in at the shelter. It was painful to leave my home, but I was not willing to be verbally or physically abused by anyone ever again. So right after the lady at the shelter took us to our room and after I put my daughter to sleep, I received a phone call. The county firm was offering me a job paying $28.40 an hour. I can honestly say that the moment I stepped out on faith with nowhere to go, God showed up and blessed me with a position I was not even qualified for!

Although the position I was hired for was a temporary one-year position, the organization was also trying to create another position just to keep me on board after the term ended. During that transition, I ended up at another location within the organization and there was where the turnaround got real for me.

Chapter Twelve

THE ACCIDENT

Isaiah 38:16-17 KJV

"You restored me to health and let me live. Surely it was for my benefit that I suffered such anguish. In your love you kept me from the pit of destruction; you have put all my sins behind your back."

Crystal is an old friend I have known for at least thirty plus years, and I've spoken about earlier in the first chapter. We were talking on the phone one day and then decided to go to the casino. The casino was only fifteen minutes away from where she lived at the time. Crystal's boyfriend, whom was locked up in a rehabilitation center at the time, needed us to stop at the bank first to add money to his account before we left. Once I pulled into the bank parking lot, Crystal stated she did not want to go inside and wanted me to pull up at the drive-thru window.

As I exited the bank parking lot, I stopped at the corner stop sign. Traffic was literally backed up bumper to bumper for blocks. The lady in the first lane saw me trying to make a left turn and hand gestured me to go across in front of her vehicle. I approached the second lane I needed to cross in order to get to the median lane. The truck in the second lane gave me the okay to move forward across his lane in front of his vehicle.

The man driving the truck in the second lane, motioned me to go for it towards the median turning lane. Something told me to brake really hard, pull myself up onto the steering wheel closest to the windshield to see clearly around the second lane first! Before I could wrap eyes around the second lane to see if anyone was coming, a small BMW came speeding down the median out of nowhere. The car clipped my passenger headlight and dragged me a few inches down the median lane. The impact was so hard, my hands were still holding on the steering wheel and I felt a ripping tear. I had to let go quickly or my arms would have been snatched from my body.

That particular day, I was supposed to drop my mom off at the airport later that afternoon. So, after all the reports were made, I called my mom to come pick us up. My mom still needed to be dropped off at the airport, so Crystal and I rode with her to drive my mom's car back. Once Crystal and I arrived at Crystal's home, I began to feel pain in my lower back and shoulders. But still wanting to go to the casino, we went anyway in spite of everything we just went through.

As we gambled, I began to feel pain everywhere and after a while, I decided to just take her home then go home myself to recuperate. About three days later, I was in so much pain I jumped up and drove myself straight to the hospital. I eventually had a few MRI's and discovered that there were multiple injuries and I needed help. Two pinched nerves in my neck and back, two torn rotator cuffs, and numerous herniated and ruptured disks up and down my spine.

I can remember thinking, why is my pain in the shape of the cross Jesus died on? From the center of the back of my head, down my neck, to the lower back, and across shoulder to shoulder. It seemed as though I was being crucified. The pain was the greatest pain I had ever felt in my entire life. Out of my cry for help, my relationship with the Lord deepened.

Sleep was only granted in the daylight, and the night hours was filled with tears of pain and discomfort. It was so unbearable that I made a promise to God that if he'd take the pain away, I would serve Him even more. I begged the Lord over and over, "What is it you want from me?" What did I do to be made to suffer so painfully without sleep?" In those moments, I would rather have died than suffer another night.

One day, I was scrolling down the YouTube newsfeed and saw an interesting video title from an Apostle, Gino Jennings. The title of the video was called, "Marriage, Divorce, and Remarriage." As I listened to the Pastor's sermon, I couldn't believe what I was hearing. He simply explained marriage and why divorce was man-made and not so in the eyes of God. My ears could not believe what I was hearing.

The bible says, I belong to my husband until death. Even today after we've divorced already. My soul began to search the scriptures through and through for a way out of this marriage that I thought was over twenty years ago. The bible says that death is the only way out of a marriage, and I shall only be separated in God's eyes. The Bible also says that I shall not be with another man until my first husband has passed away from this earth and that I shall live alone until then without reconciliation to the same man I married. My heart seemed to have burst wide open and I became very depressed and angry.

The emotions I was feeling at that time had provoked me to consider contacting my ex-husband. I was so upset that he asked me to marry him and then just walked away like it meant nothing to him or God. I couldn't imagine someone turning their back on God in this way if they knew the truth about the way the Lord really felt about marriage. My mind was going one hundred miles an hour while trying to contact this man on any and every social media I could find.

Mind you, he had been married to another woman for over fifteen years at that time. I sent him and his so-called wife several messages on Facebook with the scriptures and videos from the Apostle. Talk about going crazy! Somehow, I thought that when he heard the Apostle's sermon, he'd be spiritually shocked as well and maybe willing to at least talk to me about it. Obviously, the man had been married for over fifteen years to another woman, and he was not trying to hear from me at all. I must've sounded like a lunatic after all the years we had been apart.

I also told his so-called wife that the Bible said I was still his wife and she was married to another woman's husband! Moreover, I then went on to say that the Bible also called her a whore for sleeping with another woman's husband and that I would fast and pray till this earth's end for my husband to come back to me. When I visited her father's page, I immediately noticed that he had a video of my Pastor on his timeline. The video on her dad's timeline was a sermon about imagery and idol worshipping. In that moment, I just knew her dad would understand my intrusion and persuade his daughter to give up my man.

Yeah right! I posted a message on the father's page right up under the video of my pastor on his timeline. It read, "Apostle Gino really knows his stuff! He also teaches about Marriage, Divorce and Remarriage". I then went on to say, "He helped me realize that I still belong to my husband even though we have been divorced for over fifteen years now. After I confirmed this with scripture, I decided to contact my ex-husband and ask for a reconciliation. I still love my husband and I will continue to fast and pray for my husband to return back home to me."

I also added that my husband's name is blah blah blah and my name and signed God Bless You and may God also give you the desires of your heart as well. Yep, but I was sure the praying, believing

Christians would hear and submit to the word of God. Boy was I wrong. They all blocked me on every social media page I could find and disappeared in cyber space. All except for the so-called wife. But after I spoke my peace, there was no need to contact either of them ever again.

Now, I know I was wrong for contacting them and trying to disrupt their home, because my faith tells me to look to the hills whence comes my help. God is in charge and capable of all things and doesn't need any help from me. The pain was real, though from the inside out and I needed something to give right away. So, I continued to listen to the Apostle Gino Jenning's sermons and learned about Holy fasting and the promises of God, and that was when I decided to go on my very first Holy Fast unto the Lord.

My Holy Fast started from six am until around 10pm. First, I anointed my head with oil, and said a pray to inform God what I was doing, why, and for how long I was doing it. So, for about sixteen hours, I saturated myself in the Word of the Lord and Prayer. No gum chewing, no food, no water and no outside entertainment or conversation outside the word of God. No cell phone usage and no TV watching unless it was a sermon from a man of God.

It was a bit challenging, having a child in the home and needing to go to the store for something. But I kept the Word of God in my ear the entire time until my fast was over and kept it very short with my child as much as possible with written notes.

Can you believe I had my cigarettes, a half of a blunt (marijuana), and a pop waiting for me after I was done with my fast? At ten o'clock pm, I thanked the lord for allowing me to make it through and asked if he could remove every feeling I had in my heart for my ex-husband. I just wanted to be free from the pain of divorce and the reality of being restricted from men until death or marital reconciliation. I knew my husband would not return back to me and I just wanted the hurt and pain to go away for once and for all.

The moment I completed my Holy Fast and ended my prayer, I reached for those dreadful cigarettes. I lit it and took my first puff and almost choked to death. I couldn't believe it. I had been smoking for over twenty-five years off and on. How could this be that I could not inhale without choking my lungs out? I thought to myself that maybe I needed to eat something or drink a beverage to coat my throat first. After eating then drinking the pop, I tried to puff again on the cigarettes and I choked again and it was so nasty tasting I almost threw up!

"Had God delivered me from smoking?" I tried again to smoke that cigarette and the same thing happened again and, I finally threw it away and never touched another cigarette after that moment. So yeah, I went into a Holy Fast, trying to stop loving my ex-husband, and ended up stopping smoking completely! Hallelujah! Thank you, Lord. I still wanted my husband, but I began to see this waiting period in a new light. With a different perspective, I was shown in the Holy Spirit that

God loves me and would never hold back a good thing from me. He started to show me that he has given me a second chance after all.

Another chance to be more like him and then he shall give you the desires of your heart, if they are of God's plan and will for my life. Then I prayed for God to give me desires that pleased Him and not of my own. The whole time I was being told by doctors that I would need three surgeries, and they had given me a grocery bag full of medications. I needed God to not only heal my heart but also heal my body. It was the lowest in spirit I had ever been in my life.

At one point, I could barely walk and used a cane to get around the house. My daughter's school was only two blocks down and one block over and it was very difficult walking my daughter to school. A walk that should've only taken five to ten minutes, took me about thirty to forty-five minutes. I was so disappointed in all my family. I just thought that they should be there for me in my time of need. Even my mom told me that she was not my caretaker, and I should have never taken my friend anywhere, knowing I had other obligations to her that day.

I would get very sharp pains in my side with every step I took, but through rain, sleet, and snow, I walked my baby to school every day. There was something inside of me, after that Holy Fast, that made me start to fight back against all the negativity that was going on around me. I started reading my bible more and more, searching for small ways to please God while still hoping for a miracle.

I would call my dear friend/Sista, Ne-Ne, and ask her questions about her illness and how she was handling hers. Ne-Ne had Lupus and she would be in and out of the hospital constantly. The whole twenty-five years I'd known her she had never complained or cried about her pain or discomfort. I remember asking her how she did it? I told her I'd rather die than to suffer in pain for the rest of my life. She told me that giving up was not an option. She had to be there for her kids, and she did not allow any negativity in her space.

Because Ne-Ne had already survived open heart surgery, a complete hip replacement, and chronic body pain since the age of fifteen, I believe I began to fight harder and harder ever since she told me that. Maybe two weeks later, Ne-Ne called me, saying she was going in to her first dialysis treatment appointment. It had taken such a long time to prepare her for the process. Sadly, Ne-Ne arrived and after being hooked up to the dialysis machine, the nurses noticed some irregular heartbeats and suggested she go to the hospital immediately. The dialysis center transported her to the nearest hospital that day.

Ne-Ne called me the moment she got a room and a phone. She told me that the doctor was saying that her heart valve was leaking again. She explained to me and the doctors that she was feeling fine and she didn't want to spend her birthday in the hospital. Her birthday was on July 18: just a few days away. Ne-Ne stayed until her birthday and the doctors released her on that day.

All Ne-Ne wanted to do was spend some time with her boo cup, James. James was my cousin, and had been dating Ne-Ne off and on for over twenty something years. We were friends for over ten years before I had known Ne-Ne was dating my cousin. I will never forget; I was visiting Ne-Ne one day at her apartment and my cousin, James, just came up from the basement from cutting hair and walked right into me. I was in complete shock! I had no idea that Ne-Ne knew my cousin from high school and had been messing around for years well before I knew her.

I believe one of Ne-Ne's daughters drove her home to where James was. James then drove Ne-Ne around the neighborhood for a few hours because she was in too much pain to get out of the car. But it was the perfect birthday gift for her. She loved James past everyone's understanding and her family was not happy about that. No sooner than the night's end, Ne-Ne wasn't feeling well at all and was rushed back to the emergency room.

When she arrived this time, she called me and said they were running more tests and she was waiting to see what the results were. We talked and prayed and talked and prayed. I remember her asking me why God was allowing this to happen? I told her, "I'm not sure. But, If God was taking you through it, it had to be for a good reason."

We also prayed for understanding, strength, and confidence in His word to endure whatever God has called us for. After several more tests, sadly, it was not only the heart valve they had repaired almost ten years ago, but both of her heart valves were leaking. For the first time, I heard Ne-Ne say she was tired and she wanted to go home. I explained to her we had to see what the heck could be done before she left. She said again, "I got to get out of here. I'm ready to go home now!"

The doctors and some of her family began to enter her room, and she said, "You coming down when you get a chance?" I knew immediately! Because she'd never asked me to come to the hospital to see her. When she had open heart surgery, she only called me for a quick prayer. I replied, "Yes. I will see you soon." I immediately hung up the phone and began to cry my eyes out.

I tried to get my mom to go to the hospital with me, but she wouldn't go and I stalled as long as I could. My heart was telling me it was almost her time. I was so afraid to go see her because I knew when she looked into my eyes, she would see my fear and know her fate. I called her the next day, and her phone just rang and rang. I called the next day and had the same experience.

After the third day, I got a call from James. He told me that Ne-Ne was not getting any better and that if I wanted to see her, I'd better come now. He said that he had a ride and he would come pick me up to go see her. After his call, I got a call from her daughter as well. She told me that the doctor said there was nothing more they could do, and that if I wanted to see her, that I better come now because they didn't know how much longer she had to live. Then she stopped and said, "I don't know what to do without my mom," and started crying. My heart just crumbled because this is the second time, I heard the sound of a child watching her mother die. It was three in the morning when I arrived at the hospital, and I told James to go on home because I knew I wasn't going to leave her side for a while. It was the longest walk to her hospital bed. My daughter, Portia, and I entered the room and saw her laying there, seemingly asleep.

I walked toward her bed and began to call her name, and she instantly lifted up from her bed. It looked as if she was trying to follow my voice and our shadows. It was like she was blind but looking in our direction. Portia said hi and she turned her head toward Portia, her eyes were wide open. It was a blank stare in her eyes, and I reached to grab her hand to tell her I was there. She then laid back, closed her eyes, and fell into a deep sleep.

Her chest rose up and down aggressively like her heart was pumping too hard. I looked at her, grabbed my hat from my head, and just slammed it to the floor in anger. I felt angry that this was happening to her and I had not come earlier when she was still able to talk to me. All I could do was pray. I had no words for prayer, though, so I prayed in my Holy language unto the father on her behalf. I prayed until I felt God's presence and anointing power touch me and bring me to tears.

It was a feeling of despair and sadness that I could not fight against in that moment. After about an hour or so, I go out into the family waiting area and I noticed no one was talking to me. I wasn't ready to talk either, so I sat there with them for hours. Until one of the aunts asked me who I was. When I started to explain, she cut me off and said, "We are grieving right now. We know that you are the cousin of the man she was with, and we don't like him." She went on to say that she was sorry but while they were grieving, they don't care to be around any of his family. Then she asked where he was.

I tried to explain that I told James to go home because he was trying to move and I didn't know how long I would be. They were pissed that James dropped me off and did not come inside to see Ne-Ne. I also told them that she told me she loves him and that was it. I respected that, and they should, too. The family all gathered on the other side away from me, and I just cried right there in front of all of them. I couldn't believe her family was treating me like that. I loved her so much and even her children knew that, but they were not there at the time.

I tried calling everybody I could to come get me from the hospital. I remembered I had an aunt who lived close by, and I called her and she came to take me back home. Mind you I was in excruciating pain and I had to sleep on the hospital couch in the family waiting area for at least eight of the hours I was there. Eventually, my aunt came to the hospital and picked me up.

My cousin had gone back to their apartment and moved all of his things out. He actually did that out of fear that the family would lock him out and take everything from him that Ne-Ne and he bought together. But the moment they noticed he moved out, they were furious and went up to his job, intending to seriously hurt him. They even called me, looking for him. All of a sudden, I was getting blocked on social media by all her family members.

Her two daughters and sister, whom I loved and loved me, too, so I thought, blocked and deleted me first. I was checking mutual friends' pages to get funeral information. Unknown to me, I was not invited. I had never felt that kind of pain before. I was not invited to one of my best friend's funeral because she dated my cousin and the family hated him. I was in so much pain, physically and mentally. All I could do was pray, asking Ne-Ne to rest and not be mad at her family. I prayed and told Ne-Ne that we had our times, prayers and said our goodbyes in that hospital room. I'm with you in spirit, baby, forever.

I told her spirit to rest easy, baby. Your family is grieving, and I am okay and I will keep prayer over her daughters. They had a beautiful funeral without me, and everyone wore pink, black, and white. I wish I could be there, but I guess God had better plans for us. Until we meet again, my friend/Sista, I miss you and I love you, girl. R.I.P. Tanisha Lavette Patty 07/18/1972-08/02/2017.

During that time, I heard a song by one of my favorite gospel artists. It gave me the feeling that God was making changes for the good of those who loved him. I knew that God was healing her children and her family. Every time I heard this song, "Change Me" my heart cries out for my dear friend and her grieving family. Change me oh

God, make me more like you. Wash me through and through! Glory to God Hallelujah!

Slowly but surely, I started to change the way I dressed and the way I talked to people. Greeting others with love and kindness at all times and praying for those in need such as myself. First thing I learned to pray for after my accident, was for others suffering from disabilities. God revealed to me the pain of the disabled through my own limitations. My heart was heavy when I noticed how I never even paid disabled individuals that much mind. I would always pray for them but then hurry before I had to do too much work to help them.

This new awareness brought forth many tears and so, I began to seek out the disabled and mentally challenged individuals in pain or need. Inquiring about their day and asking how they were feeling. It was all I ever needed and wanted from my family and friends as well. It showed me who I could count on and who I could not. My life had changed drastically since the accident, and I can only say, "If it had not been for the Lord who was on my side, where would I be? I Thank you, Lord! For hearing my cry, changing my mind, healing my body, saving my life, and giving me a new way of walkin' and a new way of a talkin'!"

Chapter Thirteen

ENCOUNTERS WITH JEZEBEL SPIRITS

Acts 2:38 KJV

"Then Peter said unto them, Repent, and be baptized every one of you in the name of Jesus Christ for the remission of sins, and ye shall receive the gift of the Holy Ghost."

As I said earlier in the first chapter, I have always had a fascination with the church as far as I can remember. It was the only place in the world that I felt I fit in perfectly. At least up until I opened my mouth, of course. Speaking of opening my mouth, I did just that all the time it seems. Because of my free-spirited nature, it was easy for me to openly worship the Lord in spirit and in truth with all my heart and soul.

The problem was that when others saw me worship the Lord, it seemed to have an effect on them and they would instantly start blessing me with things and befriending me. The women would start bringing me things to the church and the men would stare from across the room with amazement and attraction in their eyes. I would find myself sitting in church trying to rebuke the thoughts running through my mind when I looked in the eyes of many.

There was a church I once attended where they taught us how to praise the lord with dance. I was a bit shy when it came to crying in public, and this particular church helped me with that. They did this thing where they would run around the sanctuary during praise and worship time. As I jogged around the sanctuary, it helped me to put the insecurities down and concentrate more on Jesus! I would just close my eyes and shout out to the Lord for help! It was okay because no one could hear me due to everyone else running and shouting at the same time.

As I became more and more comfortable with praising God publicly, the assistant pastor there once again became fascinated with the anointing on my life. He heard me sing one day and then asked me if I would sing a solo for the upcoming event. It was a delight for me, but the choir

members were pissed! They began to speak on the policy and procedure process to join and sing in their choir.

It was explained to me that you must complete new members class before joining the choir. It would be another set of rehearsals and other compliances before you were given a solo. When brought to the assistant Pastor's attention, he respectfully told them that he wanted me to sing and that was it! It was becoming clearer that the choir members had issues and it wasn't long before the wife took notice. Pastor's wife had her eye on me and began with the starring and withdrawn demeanor toward me.

Shortly after that discussion with the choir members, I began to receive small gifts and gestures that made me start to question his motives. However, the more attention the assistant pastor gave me, the more uncomfortable I became. It's hard to explain, but that kind of flirtatious attention that can make you feel a bit awkward in the presence of his wife. Moreover, I even felt embarrassment for the wife as she hid in the back corner, listening and staring with a blank look on her face. Constantly feeling like I was being watched and even sabotaged at times.

When seeing the look of sadness and defeat in anyone's eyes, it caused me to feel a need to be a bit more inclusive and inviting. I felt obligated to reassure the wives that I had no interest at all in their husbands. Once it became heavy and burdened, I would eventually move on to another church until I actually found one that I believed was a perfect fit for me. But yeah, it got much worse before it got better.

This one particular church, the pastor watched me worship the Lord and then started preaching how everyone needed to pray and worship a little more and really give God your all as if he was using me as the model. Then he started giving me the microphone to speak or using me as the illustration in his sermons. I began to feel uncomfortable especially when I turned to look back at his wife and she seemed sad and very threatened by my presence. You know when you can feel the eyes of a man's wife searching you for any signs of attraction. She had a look in her eyes that I could not ignore.

For some reason I felt like he did this to every pretty face that walked through the door based off his wife's disposition way in the back of the church. He never mentioned his wife at all, and his sermons were mostly about wives slacking on their job and needing to get better with their responsibilities. His sermons were so transparent that I was completely embarrassed for her. After so many sermons on wives being better and more appreciative of their husbands and how other women were lined up to take their places, I eventually stopped attending their services. There was no way I could allow myself to be the image in someone's wife's head as a threat or someone that brings pain to another's life period.

Simply because I knew the pain of loving someone that didn't quite love you the same way, and the feeling of jealousy due to a husband's attention seeking traps. Moreover, it really breaks my heart actually. The thought of my husband making me feel insecure around other women was just heartbreaking. I have a special passion and concern for marriages due to the Word of God and also because my marriage ended so abruptly. I will spend the rest of my life respecting and honoring all marriage covenants joined with God because I still believe in the sanctification of covenants entered in with God.

Marriages are sacred to the Lord, and if I were you, I would never touch what God has brought together and let no man put asunder till death do you part! I truly believe this, and it has shown to be true in my life for sure! It was not the first or last time a pastor made me feel uncomfortable in the presence of his wife but I will continue to honor my sisters in Christ and continue to serve the Lord in spirit and in truth. The mentions of these Jezebel experiences are not to defile or degrade the church in any way whatsoever. My goal is to be completely transparent and honest about the things I've experienced and that no one else seems to talk about honestly, anyway.

My next experience with the Jezebel spirit was a little different from the previous scenarios. This time I was almost overtaken by that dreadful spirit. It was a community basketball night, and I was allowing my boys to play a little with the other children there. This particular pastor came out dressed to play ball and immediately my eyes began to sin. The man was fine already, but those shorts he had on with that jersey had me imagining things that were not in the bible.

My eyes started from his feet and began to work my way up very slowly. The man was incredibly attractive but also newly widowed. Once my eyes passed his waist and began to reach his face, Bam! He caught me! He was staring at me the whole time, waving me to come over to him and I was in lala land for a moment while lusting after him in my mind. I was so ashamed I tried to hurry and look away but he was gesturing me to come over to where he was across the room talking with another man.

When I walked over to hm, he asked, "What were you thinking about?"

I said, "Huh?"

"What were you thinking about just then when I was calling you?" he repeated. I apologized and told him I repent! He insisted on me telling him, and I insisted that I was not all the way saved yet and that I could not say these things in church house. He then said, "Well, let's step outside," because he really wanted to know exactly what I was thinking. Once we stepped outside, I warned him that it was a sin and I was sorry for allowing my mind to wander off like that.

Then I admitted that I was admiring how sexy he was and that I had never seen him without his suit on. I was so nervous, I just kept talking and talking, spilling all my dirty laundry. Then I asked him to place my number in his phone to finish the conversation later because people were coming out of the building needing to speak with him. I became so delusional. I was in awe that this fine pastor actually flirted with me, or did he? My mind told me that he was flirting with me and also that I was not all that filthy if this man actually found me interesting. I instantly thought that maybe one day I could be the first lady of a multi-million-dollar church.

The next day, I threw away all my cigarettes and ashtrays again, baby! The thought of having the opportunity to be a first lady to a man that fine and strong in the Lord was like my dream come true. I thought being a first lady would force me to live right and inspire me as well to continue even more in the Lord. After that moment, I was ready to work on me and do whatever I needed to do! I then began noticing him watching me through the very slits and cracks in the doors of the building.

I was kind of freaked out by that because he never spoke another word to me off record again after that one day. But boy did my mind refuse to acknowledge that fact and proceeded to dream on. It was the Jezebel spirit flowing all through me, that church, and the women who served and worshipped there. It wasn't long before I noticed that every woman in the church was in love with this pastor. These women had been waiting on him for years even before his wife died and were not going to let me waltz in and take their man.

My behavior changed drastically after our encounter and I was on a mission to win him over just like the rest of them. Deep down inside, I guess I knew that he lost interest for me the moment I began telling him all my dirty laundry like a water faucet, He knew I couldn't hold water and he was a very private person or sneaky one. I, too, began waiting around after service hoping for an opportunity to speak with him privately. I became very anxious and desperate. No one told me about the Jezebel spirit or the lust and temptation you can find yourself in when abstaining from sex over a long period of time. My body was tingling everywhere and I couldn't control it.

Although I am a bit embarrassed and ashamed to say, I wrote the pastor some letters that would set your hand on fire while reading. Fear was not in me at all after six long years without a man's touch. Something was in my spirit that caused me to do some unseemly things toward that man in full lust mode! I had wished someone had explained to me what my body was going through. It felt like I was possessed with a sex demon. I had never been on fire like that before except with my husband, and I needed him to touch me so bad I lost control of myself.

This jezebel spirit is deadly and every form of it should be prayed against and rebuked at its first appearance in your life. At the time, I didn't understand that. I was just fascinated by the wisdom and charm and anointing on his life. Things began to get even more out of control the more he avoided and ignored my attempts to get to know him better. The plotting and planning to catch him alone was getting real. Just like the other women, I began hanging around after service, waiting to get a moment with him while trying not to look too obvious at the same time.

With persistence, I finally got my moment I had been waiting for. He was standing alone in the hallway of the church. I only had a few moments and I decided I wanted a kiss. Yes, you read right: a kiss. I approached him slowly in a hallway. Once we were standing face to face, I began to take steps closer and closer as I entered his personal space. As our noses became so close that we could make them touch, I stared into his eyes without blinking.

I then took another step closer; he was not blinking either, staring me right in the eyes. I leaned in with a peck on his lips. That moment was awkward and after no response from him, I began to step back, smiled, and walked away. Although I didn't get a response from him, I did have hopes for another encounter. Oddly as it seems the opportunity presented itself again and yes, I made another attempt to seduce this man. I walked up on him slowly again step by step, thinking he would run from me this time.

But again, as I took steps slowly towards him getting closer and closer, he stared me again and did not blink. I rubbed my nose on his and then went in for another peck on the lips. He never said a word, didn't budge or blink. I started to feel really yucky inside. Thoughts of molestation, sexual abuse and other crazy things started popping up in my mind. I was wondering if I had scared this man to death and if I was going to hell for trying to seduce a man of God!

Because the Jezebel spirit is a very powerful one and the guilt is real, I waited some time for a response from him. But after six years of no sex, it didn't take long for me to cook up enough courage to give it one last try to get this man in my bed. Caught him again in another hallway turning off lights and preparing to leave the building. Once again, I walked up to him with that look of lust in my eyes and I decided this time I was going a bit further since I had managed to get two or three pecks on the lips thus far.

This time, when I was approaching him, he said to me, "You're not scared of me at all, huh?" I replied, "Should I be?" And proceeded to walk up on him again.

This time, well, I did the unthinkable. I reached down in his basketball shorts and grabbed for the gold. I held it and squeezed gently as I looked into his eyes with lust boiling in my body for him. Still no response, no words, or nothing. Just a blank stare. After leaving yet another awkward moment leading to nothing, the Lord began to deal with me. The feeling of guilt, filth and unworthiness eventually caused me to repent for my sins and then write the Pastor a letter asking for his forgiveness.

Weirdly enough, he finally did respond to that letter and reassured me that I did not approach or disrespect the Pastor with my lustful attacks. I approached the man in him, and I owed him no apology at all. That was ultimately the last experience I had dealing with that dreadful Jezebel spirit in the church, and I pray that my truth and testimony will help others. Also bringing light and understanding to those experiencing these kinds of behaviors in the church. The competition in the room, or shall I say sanctuary, was unbelievable, but real. I even had one very jealous and waiting woman go down to the courthouse and attempt to file a protection order on me just to have me kicked out of the church to get me away from the pastor.

As I look back on the power of the Jezebel spirit and the effects it had on me, I do understand how very few would be publicly willing to share such obscene behaviors. But my purpose of this book is to be completely transparent so that someone suffering from these unwanted spirits can identify, rebuke, and receive their complete deliverance and ultimately hold your head up high and put those things behind you and be not ashamed. I feel as though the Lord has given me the courage, boldness, and strength to tell my story as honestly as I possibly can in hopes that someone experiencing these things may find hope and joy in knowing that they are not alone and there's hope, healing, change and deliverance in the name of Jesus Christ. Moreover, just simply understanding that there is nothing that bad or too hard for God! Forgiveness, healing, and complete deliverance is waiting for you when you feel sorry for what you have done and repent of your sins.

Chapter Fourteen

WHEN GOD SAYS NO!

Hebrews 10:23 KJV

"Let us hold unswervingly to the hope we profess, for he who promised is faithful."

Another growing pain for me was learning to let go and accepting when God says No! For instance, I was working at this firm and there was a young lady named Ginger, who felt the need to police me and my work performance. I believe she did it out of concern but her delivery and tone of voice for me was very irritating. One day, I was sitting at the desk asking clients to sign in and have a cup of coffee. Until Ginger walked up to the front desk and asked me, "How are you documenting the employees that are coming in late?"

I didn't have a problem with the question. I guess I was just embarrassed because everyone in the office heard her as well. I think I was writing little notes for the employees who stated that they were in the field working for most of the day. She stated that I was not supposed to sign in for them and that I was doing it wrong. This particular morning, I was a little agitated already due to some early morning co-parenting issues. The moment Ginger started talking to me, I immediately stood up and told her, to respect her elders and if she needed to talk to me, please pull me to the side.

She responded saying, "Girl, you don't want this."

Then I repeated what she said, "No! You don't want none of this!" Somebody came and grabbed her, and I sat back down in my chair. Oddly enough, I was waiting for the boss the come in because I was scheduled to have an interview that morning. My interview was for a new position they had created to keep me on the job because my assignment had recently ended there. Right as they walked Ginger to the back, the boss walked in and we all carried on as if nothing ever happened.

Well, for weeks after that, Ginger continued to be mean and smart mouthed to me. Until one day, I had to send a client into the employee break room with her children to eat their food. After a few, the client and her children came back and sat in the waiting area near my front desk. The client then asked, "How do you like working here?" I told her I loved it there and she proceeded to say that there was a lady in the break room talking about me. Ginger walked past as she was speaking and mumbled B***h under her breath.

The lady then said, "I was once bullied at my job and I hate to see this happening to you." She then asked, "Do you want me to report her for bullying on the job?"

I said no because I was not bothered at all by her, not even a little bit. But the lady was determined to do something about the situation. My supervisor then came walking past and I nodded, stating again, "I'm okay."

Because it was never my intention to cause tension between us, I was going to ignore it all for the moment. Honestly, I still feel like she needed that redirection for future dealings with others on the job. I even wrote her a letter shortly after explaining why I said what I said and how things could be better between us and she never responded. The lady asked, "Is that your supervisor?" I nodded again, and she stopped my supervisor and asked if she could speak with her.

The client and my supervisor went into a closed office briefly and then came out looking for Ginger. Ginger and my boss went into the office. But when Ginger came out, she was crying and came to my front desk and signed out for the day. Oh my. What is happening? I wondered. Should I follow Ginger downstairs to make sure she does not touch my car in the parking lot out of anger? So, I got up and began walking toward the door, and then my supervisor asked to see me, too, but after my lunch break.

Once I returned to my desk after lunch, my supervisor asked for me to come into his office. The moment I sat down, he asked me what happened between Ginger and I. Immediately, I told him I didn't know what he was talking about. "You know what I'm talking about," he said. I explained the client's frustration with Ginger's behavior toward me.

As I was explaining, he had instructed his secretary to prepare a document. His secretary was all red in the face as if she was crying. Moments later, she gave the document to my supervisor, who then gave it to me. I decided to read it out loud with excitement and enthusiasm. The letter read, that they had the pleasure of working with me and appreciated my support but, unfortunately, they had to end my employment there with the company due to lack of grant funds.

Mind you, I had just interviewed with him for a position they had created for me in order to stay with the company because they loved me so much. I immediately jumped up, saying, "I'm going to miss you all, and thank you for this time and experience. I am grateful to have been with the team for almost two years. I walked right out of there and shook the dust from my shoes as I exited the door.

A few months later, I ended up talking and meeting with another employee who worked there also. She explained to me that Ginger told everyone that the client who told on her was my family members, who I sent up there that day to try to get her fired.

I could not believe someone believed a lie like that. I just knew that God would vindicate my name and bring her to shame. On the contrary, GOD said NO!! Although I did not do anything to get released from the job I loved, God saw that I could not grow there and made other plans for me instead, which led to bigger, better, and greater opportunities. Sometimes God will allow an unfair thing to happen to you in order to protect you and or your spirit and or to place you on a different path for his glory and your destined purpose.

It was a hard pill to swallow, but in time, it became so plain to me that I had been blessed to have been detached from that organization. Later, they ended up laying off fourteen more people in a downsizing attempt to save the organization. These types of growing pains can strengthen you, but it can also weaken you if the Holy Scriptures is not being applied to your life and every day walk. I know through my own testimony that God does say no sometimes, and we know that all things work together for good to them that love God, to them who are the called according to his purpose. (Roman 8:28) KJV There is power in the scriptures to endure and overcome anything!

There was another growing pain, relating to a job I worked at, and for some reason, the supervisor had it in for me from the jump. I could not, for the life of me, understand what was going on. I took my work home to study so that I could keep her off my head and to impress her rather than cause any added frustrations with me. Everything I did she had a problem with, and she was making my job harder and harder every day, even making sure I would have questions for her in order to proceed with the task given. Sometimes I would sit for hours just waiting on certain login information from her.

After multiple frivolous and sporadic meetings with the supervisor and manager, it was expressed to me that my employment there had ended and I was being escorted off the premises effective today. I was so tired of dealing with the whole shenanigans that I was relieved to walk out of there this time. I was not raised to just quit a job without another lined up, but I was so fed up, I didn't even care that they fired me for no apparent reason at all. As I was walking to my vehicle, I heard a voice calling my name. I looked over toward the manager who just fired me sitting in the smoking booth who just fired me.

I walked over to her, and she began to apologize. The manager stated that the supervisor was upset with her. She stated that the supervisor wanted her to hire her uncle instead of me. After the supervisor saw that I was given the position, she was determined to fire me and any other individual the manager hired. She apologized again and told me to wait a few months, reapply, and she would make sure they pulled my application again. I thought to myself, No thank you!

I already grew up feeling like the black sheep in the family, so it was even more painful to see another person lie or treat me unfairly and get away with it. I got punished instead of the ones lying and being mean to me. I just knew God would strike down on them like never before to vindicate me. As I have grown more and more each day, I can see how yes, it was unfair, but God ultimately put me in a place where he could do a good job on me as well as elevate me mentally, spiritually, and emotionally.

When God says no, there is nothing left to do but let go and keep moving. I spent over fifteen years waiting for my husband to return to me after God said No! I prayed, cried, fasted, and everything. I'd always had a hard time letting go of people that I loved even if they did not love me. My husband left me so abruptly that I was left with a hole in my soul. I did lots of things to fill that void until it became clear that God just said no.

After twenty years apart, you'd think I'd known that already. But yet some of us still tend to step into this so called, "faith mission" to start believing God for a supernatural miracle. Although everything is possible with God, sometimes he will say no or not at this time due to other extenuating circumstances. I have learned that God will never withhold a good thing from you. Trust that what has walked out of your life was never meant to be there in the first place.

Speaking of being somewhere you are not meant to be, just brought to mind this cruise ship adventure I went on with a church many years ago. It was my first time ever going on a cruise ship and I had no clue what to expect. Because I was going with a church, I just really overlooked all the small stuff but later found myself questioning why I was even there at all. Most of my time on the ship, I was searching for my fellow church members. It seemed like everyone went into hiding right after boarding.

I can remember seeing one of the married couples at the church dining from a far and I immediately headed for their table. I wanted to know if we were meeting for prayer or some type of engaging on this trip. Once I finally fought through the crowd to approach their table, they both were gone. I just stared at the table in suspense at the many wine glasses and food they had left behind, wondering, Are we drinking now?

There was no shade on the ship, no trees to block the sun, and it was hotter than an automotive production plant on an overtime weekend shutdown. The entire time the ship was serving these tall one-dollar colorful fruity drinks that were full of alcohol. Eventually, I started slam dunking them just to keep cool. I should've known that this was not a Christian ship and I had no business there in the first place, considering my history. I had about two years clean from cigarette smoking and was back smoking by the time I returned home from the trip.

Sometimes God will show you things and why they are not good for you right in the middle of it. I was very afraid of the fact that I was in the middle of the gulf ocean, on a ship that seemed to be the size of a pill in comparison to the gulf ocean surrounding us. Horrific for me enough, it didn't dawn on me until I was walking out on the deck of the ship at night and I couldn't see the sky or any land, trees or anything surrounding us. It was almost like we were just floating in midair. The only thing you could see, was the water beating up against the lights on the bottom sides of the ship.

There was no beginning or ending to the darkness that surrounded the ship. In that moment, I became frightened and rushed back into the ship with horrible thoughts of someone pushing me overboard and no one ever knowing about it. The only time they checked for passengers was after the ship returned to the US. I was glad that I had experienced a cruise, but I can reassure you that it was just not my thing. So yeah, I did feel abandoned by my then church family, which left me to party alone with happy drinks everywhere. I acted a fool the entire week. Before my suitcases was unpacked, I was dancing on top of the dinner tables with the Maître d's screaming OPA!! OPA!

From the moment I boarded that ship, it felt like I was in Satan's house. Non-stop alcohol and partying like there was no tomorrow without a care in the world. Although I enjoyed myself and I did make it home safely, thanks be to God, I think one time was all I needed, and moving forward. I would make sure to do all the research before vacationing. When God says no, sometimes you can just feel it in your spirit and know that this is something you don't want to try a second time.

Chapter Fifteen

FAMILY

Hebrews 10:24-25KJV

"And let us consider how we may spur one another on toward love and good deeds, not giving up meeting together, as some are in the habit of doing, but encouraging one another — and all the more as you see the Day approaching."

It's amazing how the meaning of love and family can be vastly different for each individual and without communication, the love and the family can be lost forever. Family is very important to me and I cannot see a life of prosperity and happiness here on this earth without being a part of one. Through it all, I managed to create my own little family and I give all honor to God for my four children now adults. It has been truly a blessed and spiritual journey being a single mother. Believe me! God carried us the entire time and is still moving on our behalf, and I will continue to give God the Glory, Honor, and Praise for such great kids in spite of it all.

I've learned over the years that family is not just the people biologically connected to you. You can also build and create the family you would like to have. After reevaluating what family means to me

and choosing to make some changes in my life, it allowed me to create and embrace the family that God has ordained for me. It was very eye opening to me to see very clearly that family is only what you make it and sometimes family may not be from the blood line. It was mind blowing because I've spent most of my life believing that I needed to fight to keep my biological family members together. I never knew that there would come a time where you would have to let a family member go in order to keep your salvation to please God.

But it was also a great relief to be able to let go of some people in my life that caused me nothing but pain and rejection issues. It seems pretty easy until those people are the ones you love the most. I now have a new definition of what family means to me and I'm sticking to it by any means necessary. Today, family means to me, the people of God! Believers of one God, one Faith and One Baptism. Those who study to show thyself approved unto God. (2 Timothy 2:15), I now know that I don't have to force myself to engage with people just because of their blood line and it's absolutely okay to pray but also let go, cut off, and shut down any kind of relationship that is not benefiting the Kingdom of God.

It feels good to have that kind of power backing me as I walk away from those things, I have left behind so that I may press toward the mark of the high calling of God in Christ Jesus. (Philippians 3:14), and only engage with people who have my best interest at heart and I as well in the reciprocation of iron sharpening iron. (Proverbs 27:17).

I have learned a lot over the years, and God is finally putting some of the pieces to the puzzle back together again even as I write this memoir of my life. As I stated before, family is important to me and I would like to share just a little about mine. Keep in mind, I come from a very private and secretive family and I will not be allowed to share much. As much as I love every single member of my family and extended family, I will continue to honor them as such. When it comes to family, I'm a believer that it comes first! Family endures, tolerates, compromises, and never gives up completely on you and I will try my best to be an example of a well-respected and loving member of my family at all times till the day I die.

In an earlier chapter, I told you that I was a sibling to one sister for most of my life. Well, yeah, because my dad had another daughter before me and we didn't meet till later in my adult years. It was fascinating how she found me. She is my oldest sister, Gina, and she is four years older than me and has three children. My other sister, Kim, has three children as well.

I have a total of three nieces, three nephews, and fourteen great nieces and nephews. I love each and every one of them and they better know it. My sister Gina was my dad's first born and she looks just like him. She even has his hands and toes exactly alike. I wish I had those pretty feet, though.

When I was just about eight years old, I can remember a mention about my dad having another daughter. It was not clear if my sister was really his child in the beginning due to his drug related issues. But unfortunately, like I said, I was a spoiled brat and I wanted to be his only child. The relationship I had with my other sister was so up and down that I did not want to share my dad with anyone. I can remember walking to a store with my dad and I made him promise me that I would be his only daughter.

It was cruel, I know, but really, I did not know what I was actually saying at the time. I told him that I did not want another sister and don't ever bring her home or around me. Not even considering that she was his first born and not me. My dad actually made that promise to me and I never saw that sister up until she found me later in my adult years. It was a call I received from my sister on my mom's side that I will never forget and always treasure as well.

She stated that she had gotten a call from someone stating that she was my sister and had been looking for me for years. She laughed and said, "You're not the only child anymore."

It sounded like she was playing, but then I asked, "Okay. Where is she? Because I knew that if I looked at her in her eyes I would know if she was really my dad's child or not. I had forgotten all about the sister I had heard about from when I was a kid. I thought she was referring to someone new.

She promised me that it was true, but at first, I declined to meet. I just felt that I would not be able to handle another sister and I did not want to be required to do anything I didn't want to do. I'm glad that my sister finally did arrange for all of us to meet up and again it was also a moment I will never forget. We arrived at my sister's house together, eager to see the face of this woman claiming to be my sister. As we waited in the living room, my unbeknown nieces came up to me and told me their names.

They were about ten and eleven years old and began saying that their mom was in the back bedroom and she was afraid to come out. I was startled by that at first and was wondering why because she said she had been looking for me for years and always wanted a sister. So after about fifteen minutes of waiting, she began singing really loud. I think it was "Open my Heart" by Yolanda Adams. She sang and sang and then started talking to us through her bedroom door. She stated that she was afraid that I would not like her, or I would think she was ugly.

Eventually, we talked, celebrated together as a family, and have become quite close over the years. My sister and I were even blessed to be there together to help deliver her second grand child, my great niece. We have bonded ever since, and I love my sister and my nieces and nephews to the moon and back. My plans are to, one day, gather them all and just share with them the importance of being a great aunt and having a good healthy relationship.

I find myself growing and changing more and more everyday hoping to become more like Christ. My life has been a journey that I would not go back and change one bit, simply because of the knowledge and wisdom that I have obtained along the way and through it all. Job 28:28 Behold, the fear of the Lord, that is wisdom, and to depart from evil is understanding.

It was only when my daughter fell sick that I began to experience a deeper kind of love between family members. My daughter was diagnosed with diabetes type 1 just a few months ago, and I was forced to reevaluate what true love really looks like as I struggle to stay strong for my little princess. The busy noises in my mind and everyday life have become still, quiet, and calm. Nothing is as important as it were before and I literally have no time to entertain things that are not made from courage and good energy. My thankfulness grows stronger and stronger every morning as I am given the opportunity to see my baby girl smile.

I will never forget the moments I was able to really cry out to my Lord concerning this. Once my knees hit the floor and I leaned in to pray, it nearly took my breath. I felt like I had just finished running a marathon and I prayed and cried until there was surely a puddle of tears left behind. I believe I left fear, broken heartedness, rejection, abuse, neglect, and any other weapon formed against me all on the floor. Because when I got up from that prayer, I got up a dietician for my daughter and a very sharp carb counter if I may say so myself.

I am writing again and pursuing, thriving, and dreaming again.

The Lord has given me my joy back, and my daughter and I are managing her condition quite well as God is willing. So, as I began to adjust to the new way of living while re-building my relationship with God, he began to remind me of how great he is! The Lord showed me a time when he used an impossible situation to prove that he is real and nothing is too hard for God. It was when my cousin Lamont was killed in a home invasion robbery and there was no evidence or credible witnesses left behind when I learned this truth.

We looked at everyone as a suspect because we just didn't know what to think. We seemed to be another family fighting for justice and praying for answers. The investigation was at a standstill and the only lead we had was a known drug addict whom was high at the time of the incident. After questioning her for hours, they eventually arrested a few people whom she said she saw last at the apartment. With no real evidence of involvement, the police warned us that they would have to release the two guys and girl they had in custody.

During this time, Lamont's baby sister, Drika, had gotten a call from her boyfriend that was recently arrested as well. As Drika began to tell him about her brother's killing, he stopped her to inform her that he was in the same cell as the guys that were arrested. Of course Drika told her boyfriend to get information from them. The guys sang like a canary in the frustration of being arrested and thinking they just met a new friend. The girl was questioned, immediately took a plea, and confessed to setting up and planning the entire robbery!

When you can't see it, the impossible, it's just an opportunity for God to show up and work a miracle! I have seen God do this a few times and I will forever place my hopes, fears, and my tears in Christ Jesus that strengthens me. The Bible says that God is love, and loves endures, tolerates, and is long suffering. Love is kind, Just, and never dies. God is Love and all the love anyone really needs. Of course, it's a blessing to have people that love you in your life, but it should never be the reason you fail or fall short of something. "His truth shall be your shield and bucker", Psalms 91:4

On the other hand, I am not my own. I belong to the Lord, and if the Lord says move, I will continue to fight to obey the will of God. I will not allow a friendship or a family member to pull me away from the Word of God and all his promises. Praying continuously for all those offended by my faith walk and also praying that the Lord reveal to my enemies and those whom lack understanding that it's not about you or me, it's about keeping my salvation! My hope is to love everyone with the love of God and to be a living sacrifice for others as it pleases the Father.

There comes a time in one's life where you begin to see the need to be set apart sometimes for purpose of growth and sanctification.

Unconditional: The Innocence, Betrayals, and Growing Pains

The transformations began by changing small things, like the way I dressed. The Bible says that women are to cover their heads when praying or prophesizing and I've covered my head ever since I read it for myself. I no longer wear jeans or pants of any kind. Some seem to think I am of the Muslim Faith, but no, my appearance is stated ever so clearly in the King James Old and New Testament versions. Once experiencing God's unconditional love, and understanding his will for my life, I began to change from the inside out over time. I have peace, joy, and contentment in all my ways. God have given me the desire to change the way I dress, and I no longer have the desires to do some of the things I use to do.

Nor do I continue in any adulterous lifestyles or behaviors that brings shame to myself or to the Lord our God. The risk of going to hell for another man that don't know how to love me is just not worth my time or energy anymore. The churches today hardly even preach about the way a woman should dress and carry herself. I haven't heard any preaching against remarriage either. It's no wonder folks are on their third and fourth wedding and the sanctity of marriage is revokable at any time.

The sacred covenant matrimony has been lost for years and it's going to take everyone going back to bible scripture regarding our lives to get it back. We can no longer be led by the temptations of the flesh but only by the Word of God. Through it all, I give glory to God for forgiveness and unconditional love, for my four children being alive and well, and for keeping me in my right mind through it all. I thank God for deliverance of low self-value, nicotine smoking, the restoring of my body, the keeping of my children and the blood that washed me from my sins and unconditional practices. I will forever serve the Lord with my whole heart and give him all the Praise Glory and Honor for all He's done for me. In Jesus Mighty Name!

Psalm 77:1 "Your path led through the sea, your way through the mighty waters, though your footprints were not seen."

Epilogue

2 Timothy 1:8 So do not be ashamed of the testimony about our LORD or of me his prisoner. Rather, join with me in suffering for the gospel, by the power of God. KJV

There may come a time in one's life when you question your very existence. When you're not really sure if the experience of unconditional love and family is even real or just figments of our imagination. Once you have survived so many unfortunate situations, you can't help but to wonder if we are even capable of loving one another unconditionally. It's an expectation that many of us has abused or even taken for granted. Can our perceptions of life, love, and family be based on a false, impossible, and unattainable experience that can be only desired but never truly or freely lived? Life can sometimes seem to have no pattern of directions or positive confirmations you can actually see, but the word of God has a way of explaining the reasons things happen the way they do. Only through God's Word, Unconditional Love, Mercy, and Grace shall we overcome and be restored and renewed back to the original state in which the Lord has created us to be. My next book will chapter these life experiences in further details and will also include more helpful information on how that particular situation affected my life, the end results, and next steps on a more emotional, educational, and spiritual growth level. Stay Tuned! Psalm 10:14 "But you, God, see the trouble of the afflicted; you consider their grief and take it in hand. The victims commit themselves to you; you are the helper of the fatherless."

Thanks for reading my story!

ABOUT THE AUTHOR

Spirit-Filled with the Gift of Speaking in Tongues and continuously learning how to live Holy before the Lord, Tawana Roquall Fultz, born September 12, 1973, served as an AmeriCorps member in her community's homeless shelter soup kitchens, Focus Hope Food for Seniors, Youth Impact Programs, and Higher Learning and Community Development for Non-Profit Organizations all over the Metro Detroit Area.

After a car accident in 2020, she developed her own product invention. Eventually, she started her own company called "B-ABLE PRODUCTS, LLC", and begin writing self-help books to encourage people all over the world.

Today, as the Lord continues to reveal and heal, she will continue to be a living sacrifice in hopes that someone will read her story and make better decisions for the right reasons according to the word of God. Moreover, hoping that awareness brings possible next steps for another to be restored back into their natural and healthy state of mind in which God has created.

Reference/Contact Info.

www.beableproducts4u.com

www.beableproducts4u@gmail.com

www.instagram.com/b_able_products4u

https://www.facebook.com/B-Able-Products-101780475156062

https://www.linkedin.com/in/tawana-fultz-6ab7b378/

www.ingramcontent.com/pod-product-compliance
Lightning Source LLC
LaVergne TN
LVHW041321080426
835513LV00008B/545